NORTON ANTHOLOGY OF *Western Music*

THIRD EDITION

VOLUME *2*

Classic to Modern

NORTON ANTHOLOGY OF

Western Music

THIRD EDITION

EDITED BY

CLAUDE V. PALISCA

Yale University

VOLUME *2*

Classic to Modern

W · W · NORTON & COMPANY · NEW YORK · LONDON

The text of this book is composed in Bembo, with the display set in Shelley Andante.
Composition by TSI Graphics, Inc.
Book design by Jack Meserole.
Cover art: *Lute with Molecules,* serigraph by Ben Shahn. Courtesy of the Israel Museum,
    Jerusalem. © 1996 Estate of Ben Shahn / Licensed by VAGA, New York, NY.
Cover design by Linda Kosarin.
Title page art: Detail from cover art by Pablo Picasso for Igor Stravinsky's *Ragtime* (London:
    J. & W. Chester, 1919). © 1996 Estate of Pablo Picasso / Artists Rights Society (ARS).
    New York.

ISBN 0-393-96907-x

W. W. Norton & Company, Inc., 500 Fifth Avenue, New York, N.Y. 10110 http://web.wwnorton.com
W. W. Norton & Company, Ltd., 10 Coptic Street, London WC1A 1PU

Contents

Ch. 15

Ludwig van Beethoven

Ch. 16

Romanticism and Nineteenth-Century Orchestral Music

Ch. 17

Solo, Chamber, and Vocal Music in the Nineteenth Century

Ch. 18

Opera and Music Drama in the Nineteenth Century

PREFACE

The title *Norton Anthology of Western Music* (NAWM) lacks one important qualifier: it is a *historical* anthology of Western music. There is a wide difference between a historical anthology and one intended to supply a selection of music for study and analysis.

Historians cannot confine themselves to studying in splendid isolation the great works that are the usual stuff of anthologies. They are interested in products of the imagination, great and small, as those exist in a continuum of such works. Just as composers did not create in a musical void, standing aloof from the models of their predecessors and contemporaries, so the historically oriented student and analyst must have the primary material that permits establishing historical connections. This anthology invites students and teachers to make such connections. It confronts, for example, important works and their models—pieces written on a common subject or built according to similar procedures, or that give evidence of subtle influences of one composer's work on another's.

Most music before 1500 was composed on some preexistent music, and there are numerous examples of this practice even after that. Whenever possible in this anthology, the music that served to ignite a composer's imagination is provided. In one notable case a single chant, *Alleluia Pascha nostrum* (NAWM 16), gave rise to a chain of polyphonic elaborations. It was elaborated by Léonin in organum purum with clausulae and refreshed with substitute clausulae by his successors. Anonymous musicians then turned some of the clausulae themselves into motets by fitting them with Latin or French texts or made them fuller by adding new parts, both with and without texts. The Alleluia group in this third edition has been abridged and made to conform to the accompanying recording both in the succession of works and in their manner of notation. (Our Alleluia set, although different in content, format, and realization, is modeled on similar sets based on this chant that were compiled by Richard Crocker and Karl Kroeger as local teaching aids, and I am indebted to them for the general idea and for certain details.)

We may also observe how Josquin in his early motet *Tu solus, qui facis mirabilia* (NAWM 33) absorbed fragments of Ockeghem's arrangement of the song *D'ung aultre amer* (NAWM 31). The process of coloration and variation that produced Luys de Narváez's arrangement for vihuela of Josquin's *Mille regretz* (NAWM 32b) may be inferred by comparing it to the original polyphonic chanson (NAWM 32a). Later examples of this process may be found in the *Pavana Lachrimae* of Byrd (NAWM 47), which is based on Dowland's monodic *Flow, my tears* (NAWM 45), and in George Rochberg's *Nach Bach* (NAWM 152), which is modeled on the Toccata of J. S. Bach's Partita No. 6. In the twentieth century the variation procedure is the structural principle for other excerpts, namely those by Strauss (NAWM 127), Schoenberg (NAWM 139), and Copland (NAWM 145).

Subtler connections may be detected between Musorgsky's song *Okonchen prazdnyi* (NAWM 128) and Debussy's *Nuages* (NAWM 131). If we compare how the same dramatic moments in the legend of Orpheus were realized by Peri and Monteverdi (NAWM 55 and 56), the latter's debts to the former become apparent.

Some of the selections betray foreign influences—for example, the penetration of Italian styles in England, as in Purcell's song from the *Fairy Queen* (NAWM 72), and in Germany, as in the aria from Hasse's *Cleofide* (NAWM 88). A crisis in Handel's career was brought on by the popularity of the ballad opera, exemplified by a scene from *The Beggar's Opera* (NAWM 90) and the English audience's rejection of his own type of Italian *opera seria*. An important stimulus both to Handel and Hasse (NAWM 88) was the new Italian style represented by Pergolesi's *La serva padrona* (NAWM 87).

Several selections document the influence of vernacular and traditional music on art music. Haydn based the finale of his Symphony No. 104 (NAWM 99) on what was probably a Croatian song. Debussy adapted a texture and melodic idiom of the Javanese gamelan to his own orchestral idiom in *Nuages* (NAWM 131). Stravinsky simulated folk-polyphony in the *Le Sacre du printemps* (NAWM 137). Bartók emulated the styles of Serbo-Croatian *parlando-rubato* chanting and of Bulgarian dance orchestras in his *Music for Strings, Percussion, and Celesta* (NAWM 133), and Gunther Schuller caught the flavors of Middle Eastern music in *Arabische Stadt* (NAWM 150b). William Grant Still in his *Afro-American Symphony* (NAWM 146) and Schuller in his *Der Blauteufel* (NAWM 150a) applied elements of the blues and jazz.

Some composers are represented by more than one work to permit comparison of early and late styles (for example, Josquin, Monteverdi, Bach, Vivaldi, Haydn, Beethoven, and Schoenberg) or to show distinct approaches by a single composer to diverse genres (Machaut, Dufay, Victoria, Byrd, Purcell, Buxtehude, Handel, Haydn, Mozart, Beethoven, and Schumann).

A number of the pieces represented new departures in their day—for example, Willaert's *Aspro core* from his *Musica nova* (NAWM 38), Viadana's solo concerto, *O Domine Jesu Christe* (NAWM 62), Rousseau's scene from *Le Devin du village* (NAWM 89), and C. P. E. Bach's sonata (NAWM 94).

Certain pieces won a place because they were singled out by contemporary critics. On the one hand, Arcadelt's *Ahime, dov'è 'l bel viso* (NAWM 37) was hailed in 1549 by Bernardino Cirillo as a ray of hope for the future of text-expressive music; on the other, Monteverdi's *Cruda Amarilli* (NAWM 41) was dismembered by Artusi in his dialogue of 1600 that is at once a critique and a defense of Monteverdi's innovations. Caccini mentioned in the preface to his own *Euridice* that *Perfidissimo volto* (NAWM 54) was one of his pioneering attempts, and Cesti's *Intorno all'idol mio* (NAWM 58) was one of the most frequently cited arias of the mid-seventeenth century. Other works discussed in contemporaneous literature are Lully's monologue in *Armide*, *Enfin il est en ma puissance* (NAWM 70), which was roundly criticized by Rousseau and carefully analyzed by Rameau and d'Alembert; the scene of Carissimi's *Jephte* (NAWM 64), chosen by Athanasius Kircher as a triumph of the powers of musical expression; the first movement of Beethoven's *Eroica* Symphony (NAWM 106) and the *Danse des adolescentes* in Stravinsky's *Le Sacre* (NAWM 137), both objects of critical uproar after their premieres. All these compositions are exemplars of "reception history," a field that has attracted considerable attention recently among teachers and historians.

Certain items serve to correct commonplace misconceptions about the history of music. Cavalieri's *Dalle più alte sfere* (NAWM 53) of 1589 shows that florid monody existed well before 1600. The symphonic movements of Sammartini and Stamitz (NAWM 87 and 95) show that there was more than one path—Haydn's—to the Viennese symphony. The Allegro from Johann Christian Bach's E-flat Harpsichord/Pianoforte Concerto (NAWM 96) testifies to Mozart's dependence on this earlier model in his own Piano Concerto K. 488 (NAWM 102). The movement from Clementi's sonata (NAWM 105) reveals an intense romanticism and creative use of the piano that surpass Beethoven's writing of the same period and probably influenced it.

In keeping with the recent interest in the work of women composers, this anthology has been enriched to include music by Hildegard of Bingen, Comtessa Beatriz de Dia, Barbara Strozzi, Clara Wieck Schumann, Sofia Gubaidulina, and Ruth Crawford Seeger (NAWM 6, 10, 60, 118, 134, and 144).

In general, the selections are free of any insinuations on the part of this editor. They are simply superlative creations that represent their makers, genres, or times. Most of the *ars nova* and many of the Renaissance works fall into this category, as do a majority of those of the Baroque, Romantic, and modern periods. My choices often mark important turning points and shifts of style, historical phenomena that are interesting if not always productive of great music, new models of constructive procedures, typical moments in the work of individual composers, and challenging specimens for historical and structural analysis.

The proportion of space assigned to a person or work does not reflect my valuation of the composer's greatness. Regrettably, many major figures could not be represented at all. In an anthology of limited size every work chosen excludes another of corresponding size that may be equally worthy. Didactic functionality, historical illumination, and intrinsic musical quality, rather than "greatness," "genius," or popularity, were the major criteria for selection.

The inclusion of a complete Office (NAWM 4) and a nearly complete Mass (NAWM 3) deserves special comment. I realize that the rituals as represented here have little validity as historical documents of the Middle Ages.

It would have been more authentic, perhaps, to present a Mass and Office as practiced in a particular place at a particular moment, say in the twelfth century. Since the Vatican Council, the liturgies printed here are themselves archaic formulas, but that fact strengthens the case for their inclusion, because opportunities to experience a Vespers service or Mass sung in Latin in their classic formulations are now rare indeed. I decided to reproduce the editions of the modern chant books, with their stylized neumatic notation, despite the fact that they are not *Urtexte,* because these books are the only resources many students will have available for this repertory, and it should be part of their training to become familiar with the editorial conventions of the Solesmes editions.

Many of the recordings that accompany this anthology are new to this edition. I have taken advantage, other factors being equal, of the improved fidelity of digital recording. I was partly guided in the choices for early music by recent published opinion about performance practices. For the Baroque and early Classic periods, I have favored ensembles that use period instruments. Although the extension of this practice to later music is still controversial, I have included very attractive renditions with period instruments of the excerpts from the symphonies of Beethoven and Berlioz, in part to stimulate discussion and consideration of this option. Users of our recorded anthology should keep in mind that performers take liberties with written scores, and students should not expect to hear every notated detail. This is particularly true with respect to musica ficta, where the editor may have suggested one solution and the performers chosen another, and in periods and genres of music in which improvisation and embellishment by the artists were expected. Compact-disk track numbers have been added (in square boxes) to the scores, and they are placed not only at the beginning but strategically within selections to aid in study, analysis, and teaching.

The third edition of this anthology and the fifth edition of *A History of Western Music* (HWM), for which it serves as a resource, depart from previous editions in that commentaries and analytical notes concerning the selections are being published in NAWM and largely omitted from HWM. However, very brief discussions and more extended treatments of some pieces have been retained in HWM, because they serve to make concrete some of the general trends and techniques considered under each topic. This edition departs from the previous two also in that the selections have been arranged in the order in which they are discussed in HWM rather than by period and genre. An index of references to the numbers of this anthology in HWM appears at the back of each volume.

Although this anthology was conceived as a companion to HWM, it is also intended to stand by itself as a selection of music representing major trends, genres, national schools, and historical developments or innovations.

The poetic and prose texts that appear just following many vocal works are given in the most accurate versions available; no attempt has been made to make the underlaid texts conform to these readings. The translations of the foreign texts are my own, except where acknowledged. They are literal to a fault, corresponding to the original line by line, if not word for word, with consequent inevitable damage to the English style. In my experience, the music analyst prefers precise detail concerning the composer's text to imaginative and evocative writing. I am indebted to Ann Walters Robertson for helping with some stubborn medieval Latin poems, to Ingeborg Glier for casting light on what seemed to me some impenetrable lines of Middle High German, and to Laurel Fay for help in the English version of Musorgsky's song.

A number of research assistants, all former students at Yale, shared in the background research, in many of the routine tasks, and in some of the joys of discovery and critical selection while the first edition of this anthology was being prepared. Robert Ford and Carolyn Abbate explored options in pre-Baroque and post-Classical music respectively. Gail Hilson Woldu and Kenneth Suzuki surveyed the literature on a sizable number of the items, while Susan Cox Carlson contributed her expertise in early polyphony. Clara Marvin assisted in manifold ways in the last stages of the first edition.

My colleagues at Yale and elsewhere were generous with their advice on selections, particularly Margot Fassler on the Mass, my wife Elizabeth Keitel on Machaut, Craig Wright on Dufay, Leon Plantinga on Clementi, Gayle Sherwood on Ives, Allen Forte on Schoenberg, and Laurel Fay on Shostakovich and Gubaidulina.

The Yale Music Library was my indispensable base of operations, and its staff a prime resource for the development of this anthology. I wish to thank particularly Harold Samuel, Music Librarian Emeritus, his successor Kendall Crilly, and their associates Kathryn R. Mansi and Helen Bartlett. Karl W. Schrom, record librarian, was a remarkable fount of knowledge and advice about recorded performances.

John J. H. Muller as adviser to the publisher on the recorded anthology contributed to this edition of the CDs and cassettes through his excellent suggestions and quality control.

This anthology owes very much to Claire Brook, who, as the former music editor of Norton, proposed the idea of an anthology to accompany the third edition of Donald Jay Grout's *A History of Western Music*. She has continued to assist in the production of this third edition of the anthology. I also benefited from the advice of Norton's present music editor, Michael Ochs, in adjusting the content to the changing needs of the field. Thanks as well to Gabrielle Karp for capably guiding the two volumes through the production process.

W. W. Norton and I are grateful to the individuals and publishers cited in the source notes who granted permission to reprint, re-edit, or adapt material under copyright. Where no modern publication is cited, the music was edited from original sources.

CLAUDE V. PALISCA
Hamden, Connecticut

RECORDINGS

Recordings accompanying this anthology are available under the titles *Norton Recorded Anthology of Western Music* (12 CDs or cassettes, containing all the pieces in the two volumes) and *Concise Norton Recorded Anthology of Western Music* (4 CDs or cassettes, containing 69 of the pieces in the two volumes). Track numbers for both sets of CDs are indicated in the scores as follows:

12-CD set (tracks indicated by boxed numbers):

CD 1: NAWM 1–22   **CD 7:** NAWM 87–99
CD 2: NAWM 23–43   **CD 8:** NAWM 100–107
CD 3: NAWM 44–56   **CD 9:** NAWM 108–120
CD 4: NAWM 57–70   **CD 10:** NAWM 121–127
CD 5: NAWM 71–82   **CD 11:** NAWM 128–140
CD 6: NAWM 83–86   **CD 12:** NAWM 141–152

4-CD set (tracks indicated by diamond-shaped boxes):

CD 1: NAWM 1–46   **CD 3:** NAWM 87–122
CD 2: NAWM 47–85   **CD 4:** NAWM 124–151

GIOVANNI BATTISTA PERGOLESI
(1710–1736)
La serva padrona

Recitative and aria: *Ah, quanto mi sta male / Son imbrogliato io*

Son imbro-glia - toi - o gia, son im-bro-glia-to i - o

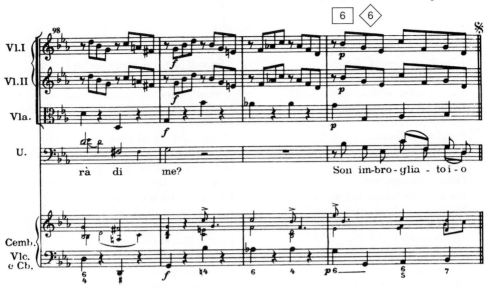

UBERTO (aside)

Ah, quanto mi sta male	Ah, it doesn't feel right—
Di tal risoluzione;	this resolution;
Ma n'ho colpa io?	but is it my fault?

SERPINA (aside)

Di' pur fra te che vuoi;	Tell yourself what you want,
Che ha da riuscir la cosa a modo mio	because this affair will end my way.

UBERTO

Orsù, non dubbitare	Come now, do not doubt
Che di te mai non mi saprò scordare.	that I could ever disagree with you.

SERPINA

Vuol vedere il mio sposo?	Do you want to see my groom?

UBERTO

Sì, l'avrei caro.	Yes, I would love to.

SERPINA

Io mandarò per lui:	I shall send for him.
Giù in strada ei si trattien.	He is waiting down in the street.

UBERTO

Va.	Go ahead.

SERPINA

Con licenza . . . *(parte)*	With your permission . . . *(leaves)*

UBERTO

Or indovino, chi sarà costui!	Now I can guess who it will be.
Forse la penitenza farà così.	This will be her penance perhaps.
Di quant'ella ha fatto al padrone;	He will do to her what she did to me.
S'è ver, come mi dice, un tal marito	If what she told me is true, a husband like that
La terrà fra la terra ed il bastone.	would keep her between the earth and a stick.
Ah, poveretta lei!	Poor thing, she is.
Per altro io penserei . . .	Otherwise I would think of . . .
Ma ella è serva . . .	but she is a servant . . .
Ma il primo non saresti . . .	but I would not be the first . . . .
Dunque, la sposeresti?	Would you marry her, then?
Basta . . . oh! no, no, non sia.	Enough . . . oh no, no, it cannot be.
Su, pensieri ribaldi, andate via!	Rascally thoughts, go away!
Piano, io me l'ho allevata:	Easy, I raised her for myself.
Sò poi com'ella è nata . . .	I know how she was born . . . .
Eh! Che sei matto!	How crazy you are!
Piano di grazia,	Easy now, please,
Eh non pensare affatto.	think no more about it.
Ma io ci ho passione, e pur . . .	Still, I feel a passion for her . . .
Quella meschina . . .	that wretched creature . . . .
Eh torna . . .	And yet . . . .
Oh Dio! . . . e siam da capo . . .	Oh God! . . . are we beginning all over?
Oh . . . che confusione!	Oh! . . . what confusion!
Son imbrogliato io già,	I am all mixed up.
Ho un certo chè nel core,	I have a certain something in my heart.
Che dir per me non so,	Truly, I cannot tell
S'è amore o s'è pietá.	whether it's love or pity.
Sent'un che poi mi dice:	I hear a voice that tells me:
Uberto, pensa a te.	Uberto, think of yourself.
Io sto fra il sì e 'l no,	I am between yes and no,
Fra il voglio e fra il non voglio,	between wanting and not wanting,
E sempre più m'imbroglio,	and I get more confused all the time,
Ah misero infelice,	unhappy fellow.
Che mai sarà di me!	What will ever become of me?

—G. A. FEDERICO

La serva padrona (The Maid as Mistress) belongs to the category of comic opera called the *intermezzo,* which originated in the custom of presenting short comic musical interludes between the acts of a serious opera or play. Pergolesi wrote *La serva padrona* for soprano, bass (a third character is mute), strings, and continuo, to be performed in Naples with his own *Il prigionier superbo* on September 5, 1733.

This scene, made up of a dialogue between Uberto and his maid Serpina, followed by Uberto's soliloquy, displays the extraordinary dramatic aptness and nimbleness of Pergolesi's music, whether in simple and obbligato recitative or aria. Uberto, a well-to-do bachelor, is attracted to his maid, but hesitates to promise marriage. She tricks him into committing himself by confronting him with a rival, who is really his valet Vespone (the mute character) dressed up as a soldier. Serpina sings a simple recitative with only harpsichord accompaniment as she warns Uberto that she is about to marry the soldier. After she leaves the stage, doubts overwhelm Uberto; each time he wavers, the orchestra assumes the accompaniment and comments at first with broken chords, then excitedly with rushing scale figures. Although this obbligato recitative begins and ends in C major and returns to it in the middle, the harmony modulates constantly, to E♭ major, F major, D minor, A minor, and G minor, shifting according to the content of the text.

The aria is in da capo form, but neither the main nor the middle section follows the Baroque-era custom of developing a single musical motive. Rather, there are as many melodic ideas as there are thoughts and moods in the text. The first line, in which Uberto exclaims in a patter style that he is confused, repeats the same music three times, reinforcing it for the listener but also suggesting Uberto's mental paralysis. Uberto then realizes that something mysterious is stirring in his heart (measure 15) and waxes lyrical as he asks himself whether it is love that he feels. But a sober voice within checks his ardor—he should think of himself, guard his independence and interests—and now a deliberate, brooding, drawn-out melody settles in F minor (measures 30–39). A short ritornello, which reaffirms F minor, leads to a review of earlier music, modulating back to the tonic E♭. But the first line's words are withheld until, twisted from an authentic-cadence pattern into a deceptive one, they bring back Uberto's dark doubts (measure 60). An abbreviated ritornello closes the da capo portion of the aria. The middle section (measures 83ff.) turns some of the musical motives of the first section into C minor and G minor, developing earlier material rather than presenting contrasting music. The first part of the aria is repeated *dal segno,* omitting the opening ritornello.

88 JOHANN ADOLF HASSE (1699–1783)
Cleofide

Act II, Scene 9: *Digli ch'io son fedele*

Edited from Dresden, Sächsische Landesbibliothek, MS 2477-T-9a.

di – gli   che lo con – so–li in – tan – to   L'i – ma–gi – ne di – quel – la

Che vi – ve nel__ suo   cor,   che vi – ve nel__ suo cor.

CLEOFIDE

Digli ch'io son fedele	Tell him that I am faithful,
Digli ch'è il mio tesoro:	tell him that he's my darling;
Che m'ami, ch'io l'adoro,	to love me; that I adore him;
Che non disperi ancor.	that he not yet despair.
Digli che la mia stella	Tell him that my star
Spero placar col pianto;	I hope to placate with weeping;
Che lo consoli intanto	that meanwhile let him be consoled
L'immagine di quella	by the image of her
Che vive nel suo cor.	who lives in his heart.

—Pietro Metastasio

Cleofide was Hasse's first opera for Dresden, performed on September 13, 1731. The libretto was adapted by Michelangelo Boccardi from Pietro Metastasio's *Alessandro nell'Indie.* In this aria, from Metastasio's original play, Cleofide, queen of India, expresses her faithful love for Poro, an Indian prince. She does not realize that Poro, disguised as his own general Gandarte (who is leading the battle against Alexander of Macedonia), is listening.

The first four lines are set in the A section, the next five in the B section, after which the A section is repeated *dal segno,* omitting the ritornello. The identical rhythm of the first two lines allowed Hasse to construct parallel melodic phrases that capture both the natural rhythm of the poetry and the hopeful sentiment of Cleofide. The unstressed final syllable of the words *fedele, tesoro,* and *adoro* result in the syncopated cadences characteristic at this time. Even when a line ends on a stressed syllable, as at *ancor,* Hasse softens it with an appoggiatura. Further syncopations occur on the accented initial syllables of *m'a-mi, ch'i-o,* and *non* through the so-called Scotch snap or Lombardic rhythm (a short note, followed by one three times as long). After a threefold repetition of the opening rhythm, these destabilizing events contribute to the excitement and suspense as the dominant is approached (measure 17). The period that follows develops these ideas, repeating the text of the stanza and modulating back to the tonic. Whenever the singer is performing, the orchestra retreats to a subordinate accompanying function.

The title role in 1731 was taken by Hasse's bride, Faustina Bordoni, who undoubtedly embellished the written vocal line: an embellished version of the soprano attributed to or composed for Faustina survives.* An even more elaborate version of this aria, as sung by the castrato Antonio Uberti known as Porporino, survives in the hand of Frederick II, king of Prussia (reigned

---

*Published in Hellmuth Christian Wolff, *Original Vocal Improvisations from the 16th–18th Centuries* (Cologne: Arno Volk Verlag, Hans Gerig, 1972), pp. 143–68.

1740–86), an amateur flutist and composer. A portion of this version appears above Hasse's melody in HWM, Example 13.5.* This version is ablaze with trills, mordents, rapid turns, scales, triplets, and arpeggios. Such embellishments, it is believed, were employed particularly in the da capo repetition, while the singer may have held more strictly to the composer's notation the first time through.

*The entire version is published in a facsimile of the manuscript (Berlin, Deutsche Staatsbibliothek, Poelchau collection) in Friedrich II, *Auszierung zur Arie Digli ch'io son fedele aus der Oper Cleofide von Johann Adolf Hasse,* ed. Wolfgang Goldhan (Wiesbaden: Breitkopf & Härtel, 1991) and is transcribed in Hellmuth C. Wolff, *Original Vocal Improvisations,* pp. 143–68. Both Hasse's original line and many of the embellishments notated by Frederick may be heard in the performance by Emma Kirkby in the recording accompanying this anthology, which is drawn from the recording of the entire opera by the Cappella Coloniensis, directed by William Christie, on Capriccio CD 10 193/96 (1987).

JEAN-JACQUES ROUSSEAU (1712–1778)

Le Devin du village

Scene 1: Air: *J'ai perdu tout mon bonheur*

Reprinted from *Le Devin du village,* Charles Chaix, ed. (Geneva: Edition Henn, 1924), pp. 11–17.

(douleur tendre)

ces - se? Rien ne peut gué - rir mon a - mour et tout aug - men - te ma tris -

14

tes - se.

J'ai per - du mon ser - vi - teur;   j'ai per - du tout mon bon -

heur.   Co - lin me dé - lais - se,   Co - lin me dé -

lais - se.

COLETTE

J'ai perdu tout mon bonheur,	I have lost all my happiness,
J'ai perdu mon serviteur.	I have lost my servant.
Colin me délaisse.	Colin forsakes me.
Hélas! il a pu changer!	Alas, he could have changed.
Je voudrais n'y plus songer.	I would rather stop dreaming about it.
J'y songe sans cesse.	yet I dream about it incessantly.

(Récit)

Il m'aimait autrefois, et ce fut mon malheur . . .	He loved me once, and this was my bad luck . . .
Mais quelle est donc celle qu'il me préfère?	But who, then, is she whom he prefers?
Elle est donc bien charmante!	She must be very charming!
Imprudente bergère,	Imprudent shepherdess,
Ne crains tu point les maux	do you not fear at all the misfortunes
Que j'éprouve en ce jour?	that I am experiencing today?
Colin a pu changer; tu peux avoir ton tour . . .	Colin could have changed; you may have your turn . . .
Que me sert d'y rêver sans cesse?	What good does it do to dream about it incessantly?
Rien ne peut guérir mon amour	Nothing can cure my love
Et tout augmente ma tristesse.	and everything increases my sorrow.
J'ai perdu mon serviteur . . . etc.	I have lost my servant . . . etc.
Je veux le haïr; je le dois . . .	I want to hate him: I must do it . . .
Peut-être il m'aime encor . . .	Perhaps he loves me still . . .
Pourquoi me fuir sans cesse?	Why does he shun me incessantly?
Il me cherchait tant autrefois.	He used to look for me once.
Le devin du canton fait ici sa demeure:	The soothsayer of the canton makes his home here.
Il sait tout; il saura le sort de mon amour.	He knows all; he will know the fate of my love.
Je le vois et je veux m'eclaircir en ce jour.	I see him, and I want this clarified today.

Libretto by the composer

Inspired by the new Italian melodic style, this aria, sung by the heroine Colette, is neatly phrased in groups of two measures, naïvely harmonized and simply accompanied. The constant repetition of an attractive enough invention is relieved only by a dominant-key section, which gives a slightly different turn to the tune. The main tune returns once more, in rondeau fashion, after a *récit,* an interlude that is indebted to Italian recitative for its speechlike delivery but succumbs to the French appetite for ornaments.

John Gay (1685–1732)

The Beggar's Opera

Scenes 11 to 13

Scene 11

MRS. PEACH: The thing, husband, must and shall be done. For the sake of intelligence we must take other measures, and have him peach'd the next Session without her consent. If she will not know her duty, we know ours.

PEACH: But really, my dear, it grieves one's heart to take off a great man. When I consider his personal bravery, his fine stratagem, how much we have already got by him, and how much more we may get, methinks I can't find in my heart to have a hand in his death. I wish you could have made Polly undertake it.

MRS. PEACH: But in a case of necessity, our own lives are in danger.

PEACH: Then, indeed, we must comply with the customs of the world, and make gratitude give way to interest. He shall be taken off.

MRS. PEACH: I'll undertake to manage Polly.

PEACH: And I'll prepare matters for the Old-Baily.

Scene 12

POLLY: Now I'm a wretch, indeed. Methinks I see him already in the cart, sweeter and more lovely than the nosegay in his hand! I hear the crowd extolling his resolution and intrepidity! What vollies of sighs are sent from the windows of Holborn, that so comely a youth should be brought to disgrace! I see him at the tree! The whole Circle are in tears! Even Butchers weep! Jack Ketch himself hesitates to perform his duty, and would be glad to lose his fee, by a reprieve. What then will become of Polly! As yet I may inform him of her design, and aid him in his escape. It shall be so. But then he flies, absents himself, and I bar myself from his dear dear conversation! That too will distract me. If he keep out of the way, my Papa and Mama may in time relent, and we may be happy. If he stays, he is hang'd, and then he is lost for ever! He intended to lye conceal'd in my room, 'till the dusk of the evening: If they are abroad I'll this instant let him out, lest some accident should prevent him.

[Exit, and returns]

Scene 13

Air XIV*

16

MACHEATH

Pretty Polly, say, When I was away, Did your fancy never stray to some newer Lover? Without Disguise, Heaving Sighs, Doating Eyes, My constant heart discover. Fondly let me loll! Fondly let me loll! O Pretty, Pretty Poll.

MACHEATH

Pretty Polly, say	Pretty Parret say,
When I was away,	When I was away,
Did your fancy never stray	And in dull absence pass'd the Day;
To some newer lover?	What at home was doing;
Without disguise,	With Chat and Play,
Heaving sighs,	We are Gay,
Doating eyes,	Night and Day,
My constant heart discover.	Good Chear and Mirth Renewing;
Fondly let me loll!	Singing, Laughing all,
[Fondly let me loll!]	Singing, Laughing all,
O pretty, pretty Poll.	Like pretty, pretty Poll.
	—*PILLS TO PURGE MELANCHOLY,* VOL. 5

*John Gay was the author of the new texts set to existing songs. His song texts are arranged in the left-hand column, the original texts and their sources in the right. Text and notes are from *The Beggar's Opera by John Gay,* ed. Louis Kronenberger and Max Goberman (Larchmont: Argonaut Books, 1961), pp. xxxii–xxxiv. The facsimiles of the melodies with basses by Pepusch are from the third edition of Gay's *The Beggar's Opera* (London, 1729).

POLLY: And are you as fond as ever, my dear?

MACHEATH: Suspect my honour, my courage, suspect anything but my love. May my pistols miss fire, and my mare flip her shoulder while I am pursu'd, if I ever forsake thee!

POLLY: Nay, my dear, I have no reason to doubt you, for I find in the Romance you lent me, none of the great Heroes were ever false in love.

Air XV

MACHEATH
My heart was so free,
It rov'd like the Bee,
'Till Polly my passon requited;
I sipt each flower,
I chang'd every hour,
[I sipt each flower,
I chang'd every hour,]
But here ev'ry flower is united.

Come Fair one be kind,
You never shall find,
A Fellow so fit for a Lover;
The World shall view,
My Passion for you,
The World shall view,
My Passion for you,
But never your Passion discover.
—PILLS TO PURGE MELANCHOLY, VOL. 4

POLLY: Were you sentenc'd to Transportation, sure, my dear, you could not leave me behind you—could you?

MACHEATH: Is there any power, any force that could tear me from thee? You might sooner tear a pension out of the hands of a Courtier, a fee from a Lawyer, a pretty woman from a looking-glass, or any woman from Quadrille. But to tear me from thee is impossible!

Air XVI 18

MACHEATH

Were I laid on Greenland's coast,
And in my arms embrac'd my lass;
Warm amidst eternal frost,
Too soon the half year's night would pass.
Were I sold on Indian soil,
Soon as the burning day was clos'd,
I could mock the sultry toil,
When on my charmer's breast repos'd.
And I would love you all the day,
Every night would kiss and play,
If with me you'd fondly stray
Over the hills and far away.

Jockey was a bonny Lad,
And e'er was born in Scotland fair;
But now poor Jockey is run mad,
For Jenny causes his Despair;
Jockey was a Piper's Son,
And fell in Love while he was young:
But all the Tunes that he could play,
Was, o'er the Hills, and far away,
'Tis o'er the Hills, and far away,
'Tis o'er the Hills, and far away,
'Tis o'er the Hills, and far away,
The wind has blown my Plad away.

—*Pills to Purge Melancholy*, Vol. 5

POLLY: Yes, I would go with thee. But oh! how shall I speak it? I must be torn from thee. We must part.

MACHEATH: How! Part!

POLLY: We must, we must. My Papa and Mama are set against thy life. They now, even now are in search after thee. They are preparing evidence against thee. Thy life depends upon a moment.

Air XVII

POLLY

O what pain it is to part!
Can I leave thee, can I leave thee?
O what pain it is to part!
Can thy Polly ever leave thee?
But lest death my love should thwart,
And bring thee to the fatal cart,
Thus I fear thee from my bleeding heart!
Fly hence, and let me leave thee.

Gin thou wer't my e'ne Thing,
I wou'd Love thee, I wou'd Love thee.
Gin thou wer't my e'ne Thing,
So Early I wou'd Love thee.
I wou'd take thee in my Arms,
I'de Secure thee From all Harms,
Above all Mortals thou has Charms,
So Dearly do I love thee.
—ORPHEUS CALEDONIUS

POLLY: One kiss and then—one kiss—begone—farewell.

MACHEATH: My hand, my heart, my dear, is so riveted to thine, that I cannot unloose my hold.

POLLY: But my Papa may intercept thee, and then I should lose the very glimmering of hope. A few weeks, perhaps, may reconcile us all. Shall thy Polly hear from thee?

MACHEATH: Must I then go?

POLLY: And will not absence change your love?

MACHEATH: If you doubt it, let me stay—and be hang'd.

POLLY: O how I fear! How I tremble! Go. But when safety will give you leave, you will be sure to see me gain; for 'till then Polly is wretched.

Air XVIII

MACHEATH

The Miser thus a shilling sees,
Which he's oblig'd to pay,
With sighs resigns it by degrees,
And fears 'tis gone for aye.
The Boy thus, when his Sparrow's flown,
The bird in silence eyes;
But soon as out of sight 'tis gone,
Whines, whimpers, sobs and cries.

O ye Broom, ye bonny, bonny Broom,
The Broom of Cowden-knows,
I wish I were at Home again
To milk my Daddys Ews.
How blyth ilk Morn was I to see
The Swain come o'er the Hill.
He skipt ye Burn and flew to me,
I met him with good Will.

The Beggar's Opera began the vogue of the ballad opera in London in 1728. The author, John Gay, inserted in his play songs with melodies taken from folk and popular tunes, and words adapted from the originals or newly written. Many of the original songs were broadside ballads, so named for the large folios on which these songs were printed and circulated. The music was arranged by Johann Christoph Pepusch (1667–1752). The play satirized the fashionable Italian opera, and a few of the numbers parodied familiar operatic airs.

Macheath's song *Pretty Polly, say* (Act I, Scene 13, Air XIV) is described in the appendix to the first edition of the text, printed in 1729, as a "new song, translated from the French." The text of *My heart was so free/ It roved like a bee* (Air XV), sung by Macheath in the same scene, parodies the *simile aria* of the Baroque operas, in which a character's predicament is described through a comparison, for example, to a ship tossed in a storm, with appropriate musical depiction. It is sung to the melody of *Come, fair one, be kind.* Both are in dance rhythms, the first a hornpipe, the second a jig. Other traditional tunes in this excerpt are: *O'er the hills and far away* for the duet of Macheath and Polly (Air XVI); the Scottish song *Gin thou wer't my e'ne thing* for Polly's *O what pain it is to part* (Air XVII); and an old Irish melody for Macheath's *The miser thus a shilling sees* (Air XVIII). A number of the songs have a pentatonic or hexatonic flavor.

CHRISTOPH WILLIBALD GLUCK
(1714–1787)

Orfeo ed Euridice

Opera Reform

Act II, Scene 1 (excerpt)

Gluck, *Sämtliche Werke,* Abteilung I, Bd. I, ed. Anna Amelie Abert and Ludwig Finscher (Kassel, Basel, Tours, London: Bärenreiter-Verlag, 1963), pp. 55–75. Reprinted by permission.

Coro

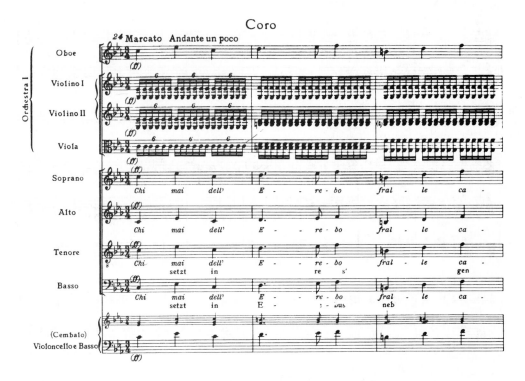

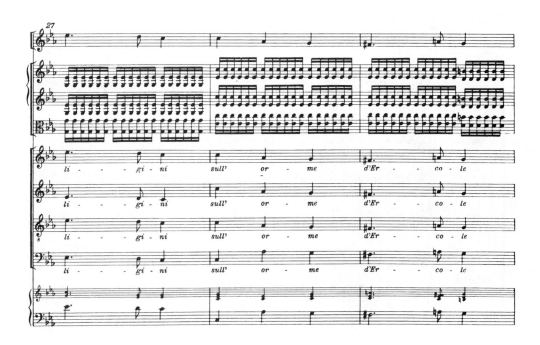

e di Pi - ri - - to - o con - du - ce il piè?

e di Pi - ri - - to - o con - du - ce il piè?

e di Pi - ri - - to - o con - du - ce il piè?

e di Pi - ri - - to - o con - du - ce il piè?

Ballo

23

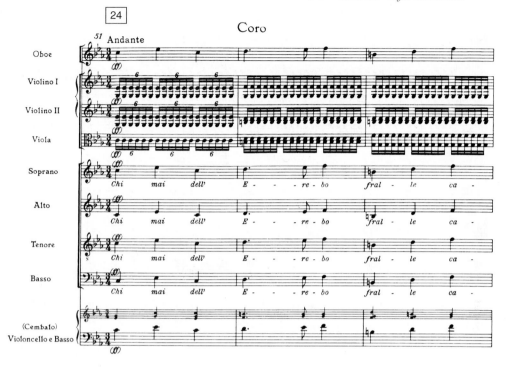

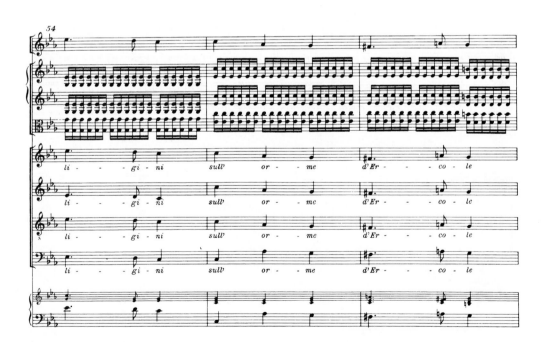

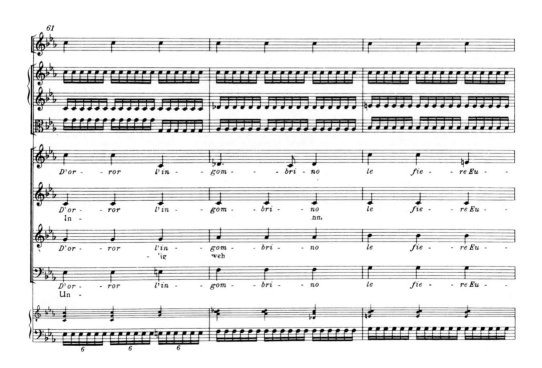

gli ur - li di Cer - - be - ro, se un dio non è!

Segue il Ballo, girando intorno ad Orfeo per spaventarlo .

Ballo

lor, vi ren-da al-men pie - to - se il mio bar - ba-ro— do-lor!

Nò!

Nò!

Nò!

Nò!

ren - da al - men pie - to - se   il mio bar - ba - ro do - lor!   Fu - rie,

No!

No!

No!

No!

CHORUS

Chi mai dell'Erebo	Who from Erebos
Fralle caligini	through the dark mists,
Sull'orme d'Ercole	in the footsteps of Hercules
E di Piritoo	and of Peirithous
Conduce il piè?	would ever set forth?

D'orror l'ingombrino	He would be blocked with horror
Le fiere Eumenidi,	by the fierce Eumenides
E lo spaventino	and frightened by
Gli urli di Cerbero,	the shrieks of Cerberus,
Se un dio non è.	unless he were a god.

ORPHEUS

Deh, placatevi con me.	Please, be gentle with me.
Furie, Larve, Ombre sdegnose!	Furies, specters, scornful phantoms!

CHORUS

No! . . . No! . . .	No! . . . No! . . .

ORPHEUS

Vi renda almen pietose	Let it at least make you merciful,
Il mio barbaro dolor!	my cruel pain!

—Libretto by RANIERO DE CALZABIGI

Orfeo ed Euridice, produced in Vienna in 1762, was the first of the operas in which Gluck collaborated with the poet Raniero de Calzabigi (1714–1795) in a program to reform Italian opera. As Gluck stated some years later in the preface to the French *Alceste* (1769), he aimed "to confine music to its true function of serving the poetry by expressing feelings and the situations of the story" (see the vignette in HWM, p. 465).

This most impressive choral scene takes place in the cavernous spaces of the underworld, obscured by thick dark smoke and illumined only by flames. There are two orchestras, one for the ballet and chorus of the Furies, another of harp and strings to accompany Orfeo's pleading with lyre-like sounds. Gluck marshals the powerful new resources of the symphony orchestra, calculated key relationships, and unprepared diminished- and dominant-seventh chords in different inversions to contrive one of the most terrifying and suspenseful theatrical experiences.

The ballet of the Furies begins with emphatic unisons on E♭, the key in which Orfeo will begin his pleading, but it soon modulates through a labyrinth of chromaticism and dissonance to C minor, the key in which the chorus opposes Orfeo's path to Euridice. The dancing Furies interrupt twice with menacing postures before Orfeo begins his song, which is punctuated with unison exclamations by the chorus. This integration of ballet and chorus into the central action of the drama contrasts with the decorative use of dance and choral music in the divertissements of the French operas and their absence from Italian opera.

Gluck also prided himself on the simplicity of his melody, sparseness of embellishment, and economy of melodic and text repetition, all of which are illustrated in Orfeo's ode to the Furies.

DOMENICO SCARLATTI (1685–1757)

Sonata in D Major, K. 119

D. Scarlatti, *Sixty Sonatas,* ed. Ralph Kirkpatrick (New York: G. Schirmer, 1953), 1:62–65. Reprinted by permission. Scarlatti's sonatas are identified by the numbers given in Kirkpatrick, *Domenico Scarlatti* (Revised edition; Princeton: Princeton University Press, 1983).

il primo tempo

The one-movement sonata written around 1749 identified as K. 119 or Longo 415 exhibits many of the traits of the genre. It is in two sections, each repeated, the first of 105, the second of 111 measures. After a brilliant opening dwelling on the D-major chord for six measures, several ideas are announced, each immediately restated. This self-parroting may be related to the habit of reiterating phrases in comic opera, making the most of witty and clever lines. It is common in early Classic music.

The ideas are not all of the same importance or function. The first, a broken-chord motive spanning two octaves, is introductory, but a fragment of it is superimposed on another idea to close each half of the sonata. The next bold theme (measure 6), immediately repeated, never returns, and the third (measure 14) is purely cadential. The fourth (measure 18), imitating the rhythm and effect of castanets, has a modulatory function here but returns to initiate the close of each half. Then the central idea arrives, in the dominant minor (measure 36). It is inspired by Spanish guitar music, with an almost constant a' sounding like an open string strummed along with those fingered. It is this thematic element that is most developed throughout the piece and that in the second section rises to a vigorous climax in which the guitarlike chords accumulate energy until they become massive clusters as all the notes of the key but one are sounded together (measures 159–68). Then (measure 176) Scarlatti restated the music that had brought the first section to its dominant close; now it is heard in the tonic.

In sonatas such as this Scarlatti absorbed and transfigured the sounds and sights around the royal court of Madrid, where he worked; one is tempted to call his music "impressionistic," except that it has none of the vagueness we associate with that word.

Giovanni Battista Sammartini
(ca. 1700–1775)
Symphony in F Major, No. 32

Presto (first movement)

The symphonies are identified through the numbering in Newell Jenkins and Bathia Churgin, *Thematic Catalogue of the Works of Giovanni Battista Sammartini* (Cambridge, Mass.: Harvard University Press for the American Musicological Society, 1976). Reprinted by permission of the publishers from *The Symphonies of G. B. Sammartini,* Vol. I: *The Early Symphonies,* edited by Bathia Churgin (Harvard Publications in Music, 2). Cambridge, Mass.: Harvard University Press, © 1968 by the President and Fellows of Harvard College.

This Presto is in a binary form with full recapitulation of the opening tonic and closing dominant sections. There is no secondary theme, but rather a transition that leads to a cadence in the dominant, preparing the way for a brief closing section. Hammerlike blows in unisons and octaves were a favorite opening in the early symphonies.

As in a Scarlatti sonata, one idea follows upon another in rapid succession, each with a distinct rhythm and texture. Only the transitional passage on a pedal point (measures 6–8) is reused before the double bar, to bring the first half to a close. In the second period, the hammer blows, now in the dominant, are harmonized and given an immediate modulatory thrust toward the tonic. After the return of the unison passage (measure 25) a new transition (measures 30–33) simulates a modulation to the subdominant, thus creating forward motion and suspense without leaving the tonic. Applying Heinrich Christoph Koch's description of a first-movement form (see HWM, p. 471), this movement may be diagrammed as follows (MT = Main Theme, OI = Other ideas):

Music:	Period 1: MT + OI		Period 2: MT + OI		Period 3: MT + OI (from Period 1)		
Key:	F	Modulation C	C	Modulation	F	Mod. (B♭)	F
Mm.:	1	6 11	15	17 25		30 33 34	38

CARL PHILIPP EMANUEL BACH
(1714–1788)

Sonata in A Major, H. 186, Wq. 55/4

Poco adagio (second movement)

C. P. E. Bach, *Sechs Clavier-Sonaten für Kenner und Liebhaber* (Leipzig, 1779). Reprinted from C. P. E. Bach, *Sechs Claviersonaten: Erste Sammlung,* ed. Lothar Hoffmann-Erbrecht (Leipzig, n.d.), pp. 24–36.

how you play is the freedom of expression

finally simplicity at the end

This sonata, composed in 1765, was the fourth in the set of six "for connois-seurs and amateurs," *Sechs Sonaten für Kenner und Liebhaber* (Leipzig, 1779). It is identified as No. 186 in Eugene Helm, *A New Thematic Catalog of the Works of Carl Philipp Emanuel Bach,* and as 55/4 in Alfred Wotquenne, *Thematisches Verzeichnis der Werke Ph. E. Bachs* (Leipzig, 1905).

German style

C. P. E. Bach was one of the leading exponents of the *empfindsam* (senti-mental) style, whose traits may be observed in the second movement, Poco adagio. It begins with a melodic sigh, a singing motive ending in an appog-giatura that resolves on a weak beat, followed by a rest. This opening is dec-orated with a turn, a trill, and Scotch snaps. Throughout this movement ornamentation serves as a means of expression rather than as merely an accessory to melody.

The multiplicity of rhythmic patterns, nervously and constantly chang-ing—short dotted figures, triplets, asymmetrical flourishes of five and thir-teen notes—gives the music a restless, effervescent quality. Measures 6 to 10 make up the transition to the relative-major tonal area, which is reinforced with the cadence in measure 14. Then in the next measure the opening of the sonata returns in the tonic and remains there while the material of the first section is developed. Sequential repetition, nonharmonic tones—par-ticularly appoggiaturas—and subtle chromatic changes assure that there is no letup of suspense and excitement.

sonata – a working form in progress

95 | JOHANN WENZEL ANTON STAMITZ
(1717–1757)

Sinfonia a 8 in E-flat Major (*La Melodia Germanica* No. 3)

Allegro assai (first movement)

Denkmäler deutscher Tonkunst, Series 2: *Denkmäler der Tonkunst in Bayern*, Jahrg. 7, 2 (Leipzig, 1906), pp. 1–12.

The court of the elector of the Palatinate in Mannheim was one of the most active musical centers in Europe. Burney likened the orchestra that Stamitz directed there to "an army of generals." The high level of discipline and technique inspired composers to demand a variety of brilliant effects.

Stamitz was among the first composers of symphonies to introduce a contrasting theme in the dominant section of an allegro movement; he opposed sometimes a lyrical, sometimes a graceful or playful idea to the dynamic and energetic opening section. In this movement from the mid-1750s, a graceful duet for two oboes (measures 46ff.) provides a pleasant relief after the rather military and busy tonic section.

The first thematic group actually contains three elements, the first featuring heavy chords and unisons, the second a tuneful soft violin motive that begins after a characteristic "sighing" rest (measure 5), and the third a horn call (measure 11). The transition to the dominant exploits the famous Mannheim crescendo, rising in four measures of chromatic string tremolos from *piano* to *fortissimo* (measures 27–35).

The development section (measures 74–107), which returns momentarily to the tonic before asserting the dominant once again, reworks the horn call from the tonic section and two motives from the transition. The recapitulation (measure 107) reviews the themes in reverse order, beginning with the oboe duet, following with the horn call, and ending triumphantly with the opening chords and unisons.

Besides an Andante slow movement, this symphony includes both a Minuet and a Prestissimo, comprising the set of four movements that became standard in most of Haydn's symphonies.

Johann Christian Bach (1735–1782)

Concerto for Harpsichord or Piano and Strings in E-flat Major, Op. 7, No. 5

Allegro di molto (first movement)

Reprinted from *Konzert Es dur für Cembalo (oder Klavier),* ed. Christian Döbereiner (Frankfurt: C. F. Peters, 1927), pp. 3–19, 22. Reprinted by permission. Cadenza is omitted.

96 J. C. BACH Concerto for Harpsichord

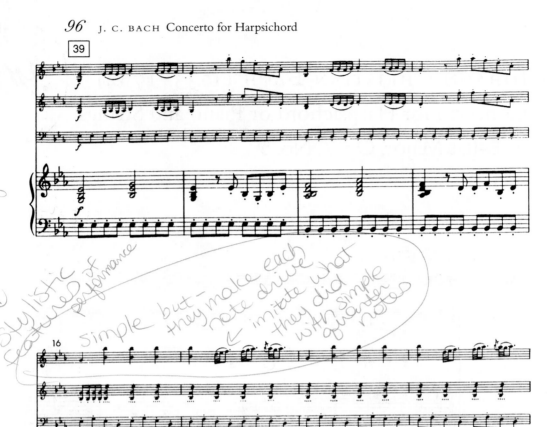

96 J. C. BACH Concerto for Harpsichord

96 J. C. BACH Concerto for Harpsichord

96 J. C. BACH Concerto for Harpsichord

96 J. C. BACH Concerto for Harpsichord

96 J. C. BACH Concerto for Harpsichord

Cadenza ad libitum

fits the hands nicely like Mozart's piano concertos

This movement exhibits many of the features that were to become common in first movements of Classic concertos, particularly those for piano. Johann Christian Bach's singing allegro themes made a strong impression on the young Mozart when he heard them in London, where Bach spent most of his life, and Mozart assimilated them into his vocabulary.

"Simple"
Still kind of sounds like J.S. Bach
not "busy" like Buxtehude

The movement begins with an orchestral exposition, all in the tonic, in which a soft opening theme leads to a transitional tutti (measure 12). The orchestra then has a light cadential theme, followed by a closing tutti (measures 24–43). The soloist now restates this material in embellished form, joined occasionally by the orchestra (measures 44–58), embroidering the transitional tutti with some runs and turns (measures 59–71) and introducing a secondary theme on the dominant (measure 71). The light cadential theme of the orchestral exposition (measure 25) fuels an imaginatively elaborated closing section (measures 85–105), to which the earlier closing tutti adds a final mark of punctuation (measures 106–14). Now instead of developing these ideas, Bach plays on different tonal levels with a new idea introduced by the keyboard. The recapitulation (measure 146), dominated by the solo instrument, omits the keyboard's second theme, going directly from the now familiar transitional tutti to the graceful closing theme (measure 171). This is tastefully extended to reach the six-four chord that announces the cadenza (measure 191), after which the closing tutti energetically ends the movement.

The parallel between this movement and Mozart's K. 488 (NAWM 102), discussed below, is striking though not surprising, since by 1770 the main outlines of the first-movement form for the solo concerto were well established. This was a blend of the ritornello-solo structure of the Baroque concerto and the formal exposition, elaboration or excursion, and recapitulation of the symphonic allegro. The tutti now have discrete functions within a deliberate scheme of thematic and tonal contrast, and the solos, though still free and fanciful, are anchored in the principal thematic substance.

score is more inviting than in the past – makes you want to play more!

Franz Joseph Haydn (1732–1809)
Symphony No. 56 in C Major, Hob. I:56

Allegro di molto (first movement)

Kritische Ausgabe sämtlicher Symphonien, ed. H. C. Robbins Landon, Philharmonia No. 593, Universal Edition, 1963. Copyright 1951 by Haydn Society, Inc., Boston. International copyright secured.

pause

Bridge to second subject

52 12

Closing Section

recording does <u>not</u> repeat

55   15

Like his previous C-major symphonies (Nos. 20, 33, 38, 41, and 48), this symphony, written in 1774, is festive and brilliant, with high trumpets (labeled clarino in the score), alto French horns (played at written pitch), and timpani. There are two oboes and a bassoon but no flutes, which Haydn used only exceptionally at the time he composed this work.

Controlled exuberance and restrained tenderness characterize the first movement, Allegro di molto. It reflects the high expectation people had for the symphony as a genre in the 1770s: that it be serious, ambitious, stirring, and impressive, yet immediately accessible and appealing. The principal subject contains three elements: (a) a two-octave descending unison sweep of the major triad (measures 1–3), (b) a soft passage built on a suspension (measures 3–6), and (c) a cadential phrase dominated by a repeated appoggiatura figure (measures 8–10). In a four-measure codetta to this theme group, a martial dotted figure turns the broken-chord unison into a fanfare.

The form is articulated not so much by cadences as by dramatic gestures and pauses. For example, a unison fanfare and rests announce the bridge to the second subject (which begins in measure 29). A chord succession from diminished seventh to dominant seventh, the last held by a fermata, heralds the second subject (measure 53). The closing section is ushered in by a playful lingering on the six-four chord that abruptly ended the previous tutti (measures 79–81). The transitions and the closing section are built on the broken-chord motive a, and, as so often in Haydn, are scored for tutti. Although the second subject contrasts with the first, it is subtly related to the c-motive by the upward leap *D–G* and the suspended *C* resolving to *B*. Thus the movement, though rich in ideas, is highly integrated.

All of the material of the exposition figures in the development section (measures 100–64). But the order of events in the primary theme is scrambled and minor keys take over. Two parallel statements of this transformation, in A minor and G minor, are heard, after which the triadic motive, now distorted and drawn out, is played against the appoggiatura motive in an excursion to the tonally most remote harmony in the movement, the dominant of E minor (measure 132). The transitional material leads to a statement of the secondary theme in E major (measure 154), now tinged with dissonance. As the strings continue to muse on this subject, shifting to the dominant of C, the full orchestra decisively breaks in with the recapitulation of the opening theme (measure 165), oboe solos now delicately coloring the soft passages. The tutti bridge to the second subject gathers energy as it simulates a modulation to C minor, stopping on a *pianissimo* timpani roll on the dominant (measure 222). But the minor mode is brushed aside by the return of the graceful second subject in major, with solo oboes prominent again. A recall of the fanfare fittingly caps the closing tutti.

98 Franz Joseph Haydn
Symphony No. 92 (*Oxford*), Hob. I:92

Adagio cantabile (second movement)

Reprinted from Edition Eulenburg, London.

This work is known as the *Oxford* Symphony because Haydn presented it to Oxford University when he received an honorary degree of Doctor of Music in 1791 (although he had written it more than two years earlier). The Adagio's cantabile theme, begun by all the violins in unison and then continued by the first violins, is harmonized simply by the rest of the strings. Although split up into two-bar phrases, the tension is not released until the half-cadence in the eighth measure. Then flutes, bassoons, and horns apply subtle tints to a restatement. The idyllic atmosphere is broken by the onset, *forte* and tutti, of the middle section in the parallel minor (measure 40), to which Haydn in a later revision added trumpets and timpani. Although its repeated chords are sharply contrasting, the *minore* interlude is built on a motive from the opening section. An abbreviated return of the *maggiore* section is followed by an epilogue that features the winds.

99

FRANZ JOSEPH HAYDN
Symphony No. 104 in D Major, Hob. I:104

Finale

Reprinted from Edition Eulenburg, Leipzig.

first theme again over dominant doublione

64

"surprise"
fugal
Stretto in B minor

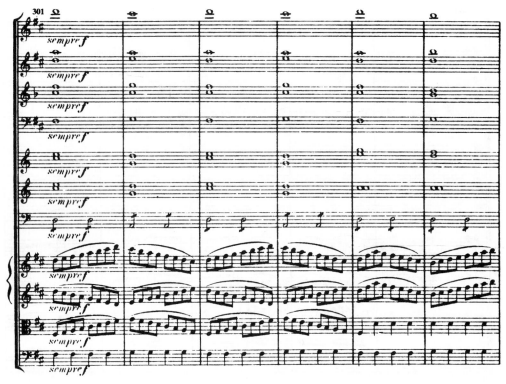

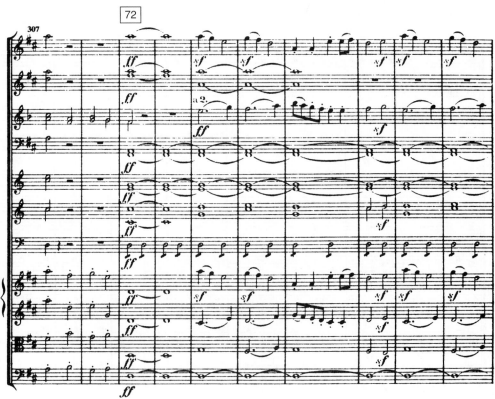

No. 104 was the last of the six symphonies Haydn wrote in 1795 for performance in London during his second visit. He had written Nos. 93 to 98 for the previous visit.

The final movement—its opening simulating a bagpipe—brazenly wears a folk-dance character. Over a tonic drone, we hear the same four-measure tune four times. It resembles a melody that Croatians sang in the villages near Eszterháza. The idea is developed in a tutti bridge leading to the dominant, but when A minor is reached, instead of a second theme, the first is reaffirmed in full orchestral dress over a dominant double-drone (measures 55ff.).

In one of Haydn's witty surprises, just as we are at last ready to hear something fresh in A major (measure 84), we get a pensive fugal stretto all in half notes in B minor, the relative minor of the tonic. This episode takes us back to the dominant for a closing tutti, the first part of which is based on a burlesqued, accelerated version of the opening theme, again over a drone bass. As a parting salute, this theme assumes a cocky new twist, which spills over the double bar to begin the development section. This and other versions of the same theme are then playfully superimposed on one another. A measure of silence (measure 166) ushers in a quiet fugal episode (now a full-blown five-voice exposition), which points toward F♯ minor. A deceptive cadence (measures 192–93) brusquely thrusts us into the recapitulation.

Franz Joseph Haydn
String Quartet Op. 64, No. 5 (*Lark*), Hob. III:63

Finale, Vivace

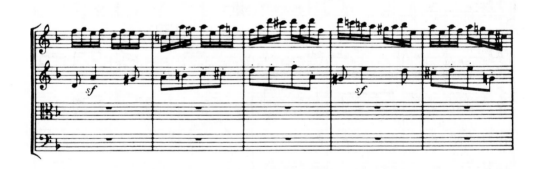

In the finales of his late quartets and symphonies, Haydn often infuses the rondo with sonata-form elements, resulting in a particularly complex type of movement. If the scheme of the rondo is represented as A B A C A B A, the refrain, A, functions as the main thematic section, the B usually as the bridge and/or a secondary thematic section in the related key, C as a development, and the subsequent return of A and B in the tonic as a recapitulation; the final A may be a closing section or coda.

The finale of Op. 64, No. 5, is a monothematic movement. What distinguishes the couplets (B, C, etc.) from the refrains in this movement are the foreign keys and the new counterpoints of the former. The couplets, particularly the central one, also have a developmental character analogous to the development section in the sonata form. In this movement, couplet C is a fugato in which the countersubject develops the main theme. The merging of the two forms may be represented as follows:

Sonata section:	**Exposition**				**Development**			
Themes:	P	T	S	K	Fugato			
Rondo section:	A	B		A	C			
Tonal center:	D	⟶	A	D	d ⟶ F ⟶ g ⟶ a			
Measure:	1	9	16	21	29	42	48	59

Recapitulation				**Coda**	
P	T	S	K	Coda	
A	B		A	Coda	
D	⟶	A	D		
76	84	91	96	103	128

Key: P = primary group; T = transition; S = secondary group; K = closing group

101 FRANZ JOSEPH HAYDN
String Quartet Op. 76, No. 3, Hob. III:77

Poco adagio, cantabile (second movement)

Reprinted from Edition Eulenburg Ltd., London.

Var. I

13

Var. IV

One of Haydn's favorite genres for a slow movement in his quartets is the air with variations. Haydn composed the melody, or Theme, for this movement as a birthday hymn for Kaiser Franz Joseph I of Austria on the text *Gott erhalte Franz den Kaiser.* The hymn later became the national anthem of the Austro-Hungarian Empire and is now the German national anthem.

In the string quartet, dating from 1797, the hymn tune passes from the first violin in the Theme to the second violin in Variation 1, to the cello in Variation 2, to the viola in Variation 3, then back to the first violin in the final variation. The variations are a study in nonharmonic tones: appoggiaturas, suspensions, and changing notes.

Wolfgang Amadeus Mozart
(1756–1791)
Piano Concerto in A Major, K. 488

Allegro (first movement)

Neue Mozart Ausgabe, Serie V, Werkgruppe 15, Band 7, ed. Hermann Beck (Kassel: Bärenreiter, 1959), pp. 3–34. Reprinted by permission of Bärenreiter-Verlag, Kassel, Basel, Tours, London.

16

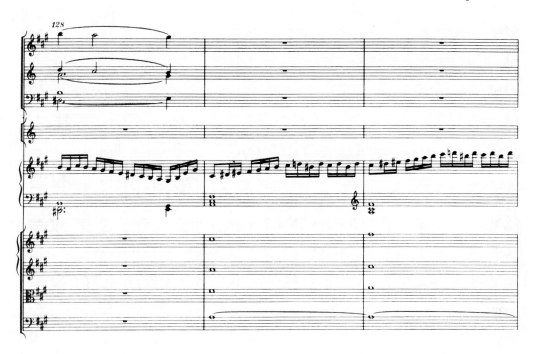

22

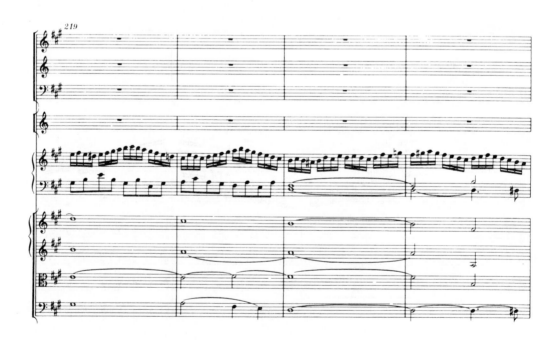

Mozart composed K. 488, the twenty-third of his piano concertos, in 1786. The first movement's opening orchestral section of sixty-six measures displays both the thematic variety of a sonata-form exposition and several elements of the Baroque concerto ritornello. It has the thematic variety and the orchestral color—particularly in beautiful passages for the wind choir alone—of the symphonic exposition. But it is in a single key and it contains a transitional tutti (measures 18 to 30) that reappears in various keys in the course of the movement, like a Baroque ritornello. Keeping the ritornello results in a version of sonata form that actually has two expositions, one orchestral and one solo with orchestra. (J. C. Bach had employed a similar procedure in his Concerto for Harpsichord or Piano and Strings, Op. 7, No. 5 [NAWM 96]). The movement may be schematized as follows:

Section:	**Exposition**								
Tonal center:	Tonic						Dominant		
Instruments:	*Orchestra*				*Solo with Orchestra*				
Themes:	P	T Tutti	S	KT	P	TT	S	K	⫴
Measure:	1	18	30	46	67	82	98	114	

Development		**Recapitulation**							
Modulatory	Dominant	Tonic							
Solo with Orchestra							*Solo*	*Orchestra*	
New material	Short cad.	P	TT	S	K		TT	Cadenza	KT	
143	189	198	213	228	244		284	297	298

Note: P = primary group; S = secondary group; KT = closing tutti; TT = transitional tutti; K = closing group

The opening orchestral section presents, as in a symphonic Allegro, three thematic groups. The first is built on a graceful, symmetric eight-measure melody. The transitional tutti mentioned above then serves as a bridge to a flowing, somewhat plaintive second theme (measure 30). A stirring closing tutti (measure 46) that also recurs twice later in the movement as a second ritornello element closes this orchestral exposition, which has remained entirely in the tonic key. Now the pianist's exposition of the first theme begins (measure 67), delicately ornamented and discreetly accompanied by the orchestra. The transitional tutti of measure 18 intervenes to start a bridge passage, completed by modulatory figuration in the piano and arrives at E major, the key of the second theme (measure 98), which the soloist now takes up. The material of the orchestral closing section is then adapted to the piano (measure 114), and the exposition is closed by a restatement of the transitional tutti, now in the dominant.

The section that follows the exposition, rather than developing ideas presented earlier, offers a dialogue between the piano and the winds that is based on new material. This section is the occasion for excursions into several alien keys—E minor, C major, F major—culminating in a twenty-measure dominant pedal point.

In the recapitulation, the transitional tutti returns once again as the head of the bridge passage (measure 213). It is heard yet again (measure 284)— with a dramatic interruption by the new theme of the "development"—as the orchestra reaches the most suspenseful moment of the concerto, a six-four chord, upon which it pauses. The soloist now is expected to improvise an extended cadenza. Mozart's autograph cadenza for this concerto and a number of others survive; many performers today play Mozart's or one of the cadenzas written by various composers and performers over the years. The same tutti that ended the orchestral exposition closes the movement.

WOLFGANG AMADEUS MOZART

Don Giovanni

Act I, Scene 5

a) No. 3: *Ah, chi mi dice mai/Chi è lá*

Neue Mozart Ausgabe, Serie II, Werkgruppe 5, Bd. 17, ed. Wolfgang Plath and Wolfgang Rehm (Kassel: Bärenreiter, 1968), pp. 64–90. Reprinted by permission of Bärenreiter-Verlag, Kassel, Basel, Tours, London.

*) Vorschlag zur eventuellen Auszierung der Fermate:

Recitative

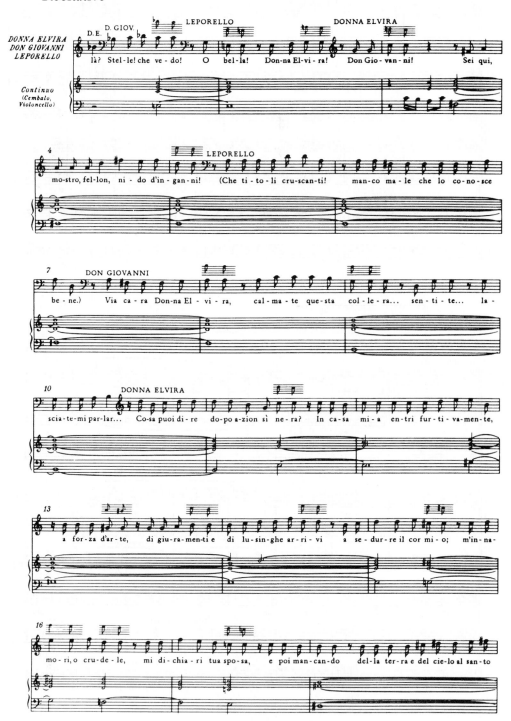

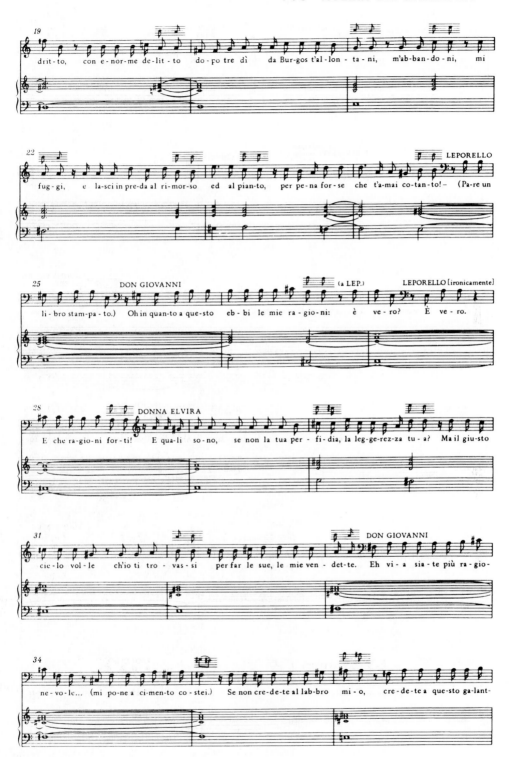

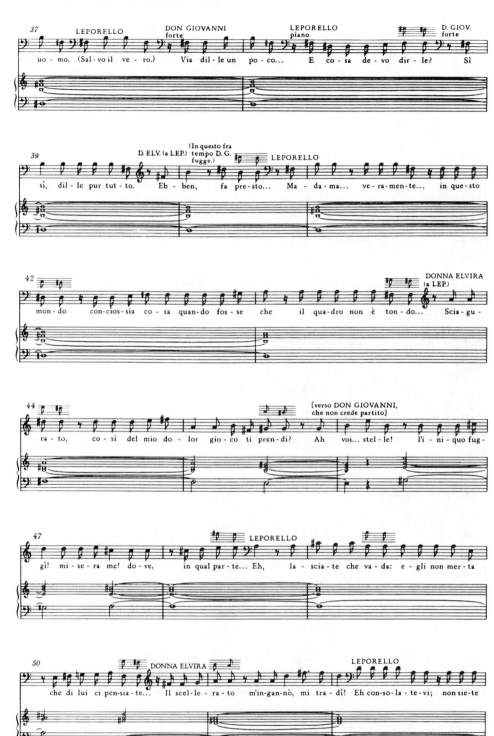

b) No. 4: *Madamina! Il catalogo è questo*

*) Vgl. Vorwort.

in La - ma - gna due cen-to e trent' u - na,   cen-to in

Fran-cia, in Tur-chia novant' u-na, ma in I-spag-na, ma in I - spag-na son già mil-le e tre,   mil-le e

*) Vorschlag zur eventuellen Auszierung der Fermate:
(I)spag-na____ ma in

*) Vorschlag zur eventuellen Auszierung der Fermate:

*) Zu einem im Autograph nach T. 153 gestrichenen Takt vgl. Krit. Bericht.

DONNA ELVIRA

Ah, chi mi dice mai,
Quel barbaro dov'è,
Che per mio scorno amai,
Che mi mancò di fè,
Ah, se ritrovo l'empio,
E a me non torna ancor,
Vo' farne orrendo scempio,
Gli vo' cavare il cor.

    Ah, who will ever tell me
    where that barbarian is,
    whom, to my shame, I loved,
    who failed to keep faith?
    Ah, if I ever find the scoundrel,
    and to me he does not return,
    I shall brutally slaughter him.
    I shall take out his heart.

DON GIOVANNI
(*to Leporello*)

Udisti? Qualche bella
Dal vago abbandonata.
Poverina! poverina!
Cerchiam di consolare il suo tormento.

    Did you hear? Some beauty
    by her lover abandoned.
    Poor girl! Poor girl!
    Let us try to console her torment.

LEPORELLO
(*aside*)

Così ne consolò mille e ottocento.

    Thus he consoled a thousand and eight hundred.

DON GIOVANNI

Signorina! Signorina!

    Signorina, Signorina!

DONNA ELVIRA

Chi è là?

    Who goes there?

DON GIOVANNI

Stelle! che vedo!

    Heavens! Whom do I see?

LEPORELLO
(*aside*)

O bella! Donna Elvira!

    O this is nice! Donna Elvira!

DONNA ELVIRA

Don Giovanni!
Sei quì, mostro, fellon, nido d'inganni!

    Don Giovanni!
    You're here, monster! Felon, nest of deceits!

LEPORELLO
(*aside*)

Che titoli cruscanti!
Manco male che lo conosce bene.

    Such Tuscan insults!
    At least you know him well.

DON GIOVANNI

Via, cara Donna Elvira,
Calmate questa collera . . .
Sentite . . . lasciatemi parlar.

    Now, dear Donna Elvira,
    calm your anger . . .
    Listen . . . let me speak.

DONNA ELVIRA

Cosa puoi dire, dopo azion si nera?	What can you say, after such a black deed?
In casa mia entri furtivamente,	You entered my house furtively
A forza d'arte,	through trickery.
Di giuramenti e di lusinghe arrivi	With oaths and flattery you succeeded
A sedurre il cor mio:	in seducing my heart.
M'innamori, o crudele,	I fell in love.
Mi dichiari tua sposa,	You proclaimed me your bride,
E poi mancando della terra e del cielo	and without earthly or heavenly writ
Al santo dritto,	or legality,
Con enorme delitto	with high crime, rather,
Dopo tre dì da Burgos t'allontani.	after three days you left Burgos.
M'abbandoni, mi fuggi	You abandoned me; you fled
E lasci in preda al rimorso ed al pianto,	and left me a prey to remorse and to tears,
Per pena forse che t'amai cotanto.	as penance, perhaps, for loving you so.

LEPORELLO
(aside)

Pare un libro stampato!	She sounds like a printed book.

DON GIOVANNI

Oh in quanto a questo, ebbi le mie ragioni!	As far as that's concerned, I had my reasons.

(to Leporello)

É vero.	It's true.

LEPORELLO

É vero, e che ragioni forti!	It's true, and what good reasons!

DONNA ELVIRA

E quali sono, se non per la tua perfidia,	And what were they, if not your perfidy,
La leggerezza tua?	your trifling?
Ma il giusto cielo volle ch'io ti trovassi,	But the just heavens willed that I should find you
Per far le sue, le mie vendette.	to have both its and my revenge.

DON GIOVANNI

Eh via, siate più ragionevole!	Now, now, be more reasonable.
(Mi pone a cimento costei!)	(She pins me to the wall, this one.)
Se non credete al labbro mio,	If you do not believe it from my lips,
credete a questo galantuomo.	believe this gentleman.

LEPORELLO

(Salvo il vero.)	(Except for the truth.)

DON GIOVANNI
(loudly)

Via, dille un poco ...	Go on, tell her something ...

LEPORELLOI
(*softly*)

E cosa devo dirle?	And what should I tell her?

DON GIOVANNI
(*loudly*)

Sì, sì, dille pur tutto.	Yes, yes, tell her everything.

DONNA ELVIRA

Ebben, fa presto . . .	Well, hurry up . . .

DON GIOVANNI
(*flees*)

LEPORELLO

Madama . . . veramente . . . in questo mondo	Madam . . . truthfully . . . in this world
Conciossia cosa quando fosse	notwithstanding that
Che il quadro non è tondo.	a square is not a circle.

DONNA ELVIRA

Sciagurato! così del mio dolor gioco ti prendi?	Scoundrel! thus of my anguish you jest?

(*to Don Giovanni, who, she thinks, has not left*)

Ah voi . . . stelle! l'iniquo fuggi!	Ah, you . . . heavens! You, the guilty one, flee.
Misera me! dove? in qual parte . . .	Poor me! Where? In what direction?

LEPORELLO

Eh lasciate che vada; egli non merta	Let him go; he does not deserve
Che di lui ci pensiate.	that you should think of him.

DONNA ELVIRA

Il scellerato m'ingannò, mi tradì!	The rascal deceived me, he betrayed me.

LEPORELLO

Eh, consolatevi: non siete voi,	Oh, console yourself: you are not,
Non foste, e non sarete né la prima	were not the first, and will not be the last.
Né l'ultima: guardate questo non picciol libro:	Look at this not-so-little book;
È tutto pieno dei nomi di sue belle;	It is full of the names of his conquests;
Ogni villa, ogni borgo, ogni paese	every village, every suburb, every country
È testimon di sue donnesche imprese.	is a testimony to his womanizing.
Madamina!	Madamina,
Il catalogo è questo	This is the catalog
Delle belle che amò il padron mio;	of the beauties that my lord loved;
Un catalogo egli è che ho fatt'io;	it is a catalog that I made myself.
Osservate, leggete con me!	Observe! Read with me.
In Italia seicento e quaranta,	In Italy, six hundred forty,
In Almagna due cento e trent'una,	in Germany two hundred thirty-one,

Cento in Francia, in Turchia novant'una,	a hundred in France, in Turkey ninety-one,
Ma in Ispagna son già mille e tre.	but in Spain there are a thousand and three.
V'han fra queste contadine,	Among these there are farm girls,
Cameriere, cittadine,	maids, city girls,
V'han contesse, baronesse,	there are countesses, baronesses
Marchesane, principesse,	marchionesses, princesses,
E v'han donne d'ogni grado,	and there are women of every rank,
D'ogni forma, d'ogni età.	every shape, and every age.
In Italia . . .	In Italy . . .
Nella bionda egli ha l'usanza	In a blonde he usually
Di lodar la gentilezza,	praises her gentility,
Nella bruna la costanza,	in a brunette her constancy,
Nella bianca la dolcezza;	in the white-haired, sweetness;
Vuol d'inverno la grassotta,	he wants, in winter, a plump one,
Vuol d'estate la magrotta;	he wants in summer a rather thin one;
E' la grande maestosa;	and the large one is majestic;
La piccina è ognor vezzosa.	the petite one is always charming.
Delle vecchie fa conquista	Of the old he makes a conquest
Pel piacer di porle in lista;	for the pleasure of adding them to the list;
Ma passion predominante	but his dominant passion
È la giovin principiante;	is the young beginner.
Non si picca se sia ricca,	He is not bothered if she is rich,
Se sia brutta, se sia bella,	if she's ugly, if she's pretty,
Purchè porti la gonnella:	as long as she wears a skirt.
Voi sapete quel che fa.	You know what it is he does.

—Libretto by Lorenzo da Ponte

Mozart composed *Don Giovanni* on a commission from an impresario in Prague, where *Le Nozze di Figaro* had been a great success. The author of *Figaro,* Lorenzo da Ponte, also wrote the libretto for *Don Giovanni*. The composer directed the first performances in Prague in 1787.

The personalities of three of the main characters—Don Giovanni, his servant Leporello, and the jilted Donna Elvira—are remarkably sketched in the trio of this scene (a). The big stride of Elvira's melody, with its angry wide leaps, abetted by the agitated runs and tremolos in the strings, contrasts sharply with the lighthearted, mocking tone of Don Giovanni and the seemingly idle patter of Leporello, playing down his role as healer of the bruised souls of abandoned women.

The famous "Catalogue" aria (b), in which Leporello enumerates his master's conquests by country and the kinds of women he likes, shows another side of Mozart's comic art. Awed as we are by the details of his characterization, by his animation of the text, harmonic shadings, and orchestration, we are driven to take seriously this most entertaining portion of the opera. The aria is in two discrete parts, an Allegro in common time and an Andante con moto in the meter and rhythm of a minuet. The first, "Il catalogo è questo," is a numerical account, and the orchestra with its staccatos becomes a counting machine. In the $\frac{3}{4}$ section, Leporello describes the physical and personal qualities of the victims. In strains of a courtly minuet he praises a blonde's gentility; after a brief pause, a few bars of an impressive symphony characterize the brunette's constancy (reminding us of the opening of Act I, where Leporello boasts of his loyalty); the white-haired woman's sweetness begets a variation on the minuet theme in chromatic thirds; "the diminutive one" is described in a patter-speech of sixteenth notes, doubled by high winds. Just before Leporello speaks of the Don's passion for the innocent beginner, "la principiante," there is a deceptive cadence on the lowered sixth degree, and Leporello pronounces the words solemnly in recitative. This short episode also has a formal function, as it leads to the cadential section before the return of the opening music. These are among the many marks of the care that the composer lavished on every detail of his comedies.

Ludwig van Beethoven (1770–1827)

Sonate pathétique for piano, Op. 13

Rondo, Allegro (third movement).

From Beethoven, *Werke* © G. Henle Verlag, Munich. Reproduced by permission.

44 40

Rondos were traditionally cheerful, spirited, tuneful pieces in a major key, but this one, from Beethoven's *Sonate pathétique* (1797–98), does not fit that mold. Written in C minor, it recalls the intense, stormy mood of the sonata's first movement and claims the rhythm and first three intervals of that movement's second subject for its refrain (see example below). This theme twists and turns around the minor third and the semitones of the minor scale. The rondo episodes (couplets) too, albeit in major keys (the B section in the relative major and the C section on the sixth degree), soon drift into the minor.

The form is transparent, because the sections are clearly set off by cadences or prepared by transitions. The transition to the first episode is especially rhetorical and theatrical, as its first phrase (measure 18) begins with an inverted dominant seventh of F minor in the manner of a recitative and ends with a type of appoggiatura used in opera. After a rest, the gesture is repeated, this time flowing into the first episode in E♭ major. The return of the refrain in the tonic is twice announced by a *fortissimo* run cascading down two and a half octaves and a long pause on the dominant-seventh chord (measures 58–61, 117–20). This run makes two more dramatic appearances, at the Neapolitan chord of measure 198, and again, after soft reminiscences of the refrain, on the awaited penultimate dominant chord of the sonata. The form may be summarized as follows:

Section:	Refrain	Episode 1		Refrain	Episode 2
Music:	A	B1	B2	A	C
Key:	c	E♭		c	A♭
Measure:	1	25	43	61	78

Refrain	Episode 1		Refrain	Coda	
A	B1	B2	A	Coda	
c	C		c	c	
120	134	153	170	186	210

After the third refrain, some earlier composers would have composed an episode different from the first two, but Beethoven, following more recent precedents, returned to the first episode. However, instead of bringing back its key (the relative major), he transposed it to the tonic, as if it were a recapitulation of second theme of a sonata form. We noted this influence of the sonata form on the rondo in connection with Haydn.

105 Muzio Clementi (1752–1832)

Sonata in G Minor, Op. 34, No. 2

Largo e sostenuto—Allegro con fuoco (first movement)

Reprinted from *Deux grandes Sonates pour Clavecin ou Forté-Piano, Oeuvres trente-quatre ou trente-huit* (Paris: Sieber, 180–).

This sonata, which Clementi composed in 1795 at about the same time Beethoven wrote his first three sonatas (Op. 2, Nos. 1–3), exhibits some of the pre-Romantic qualities evident in Beethoven's works of a slightly later period. The slow introduction packs the entire movement's thematic material into a capsule of ten measures. The movement as a whole has a broad, almost symphonic, sweep in which the individual elements are dramatized through unconventional modulations, audacious harmonies, and abrupt changes of dynamics, texture, and mood. The Largo e sostenuto introduction, for example, begins as a grotesque fugue. The subject is normal enough, but it is answered at the major seventh below; the subject's descending perfect fifth becomes a diminished fifth in the answer, and a major sixth in the next entry. A similar fugato opens the Allegro con fuoco; the slightly transformed subject is now escorted by a countersubject, and the second and third entries are compacted into a single simultaneous one. Like some of Beethoven's later fugues, this one suddenly explodes with a *fortissimo* into purely homophonic writing.

In the development section, the Largo returns in C major just after the most distant modulation—to E major—has been achieved. The subject is now stripped of its fugal garb and dressed instead in a rather common "oom-pah" operatic homophony.

The movement anticipates nineteenth-century practices in its vacillation between major and minor. In the exposition, the secondary thematic group is in B♭ major, while the closing section is mostly in B♭ minor, though it ends in major. In the development too, the C major of the Largo's return is followed immediately by C minor.

The coda (measures 236–79), almost a second development section, has the character of a concerto cadenza. Another unusual feature is that the secondary theme is recapitulated in E♭ major toward the end of the development section but is absent in the recapitulation proper.

106 LUDWIG VAN BEETHOVEN
Symphony No. 3 in E–flat Major (*Eroica*)

Allegro con brio (first movement)

Reprinted from *Beethovens Werke* (Leipzig: Breitkopf & Härtel, n.d.).

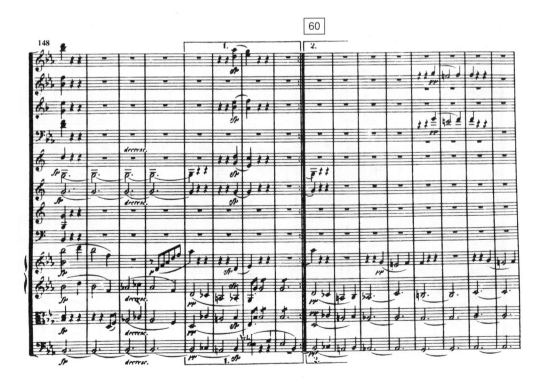

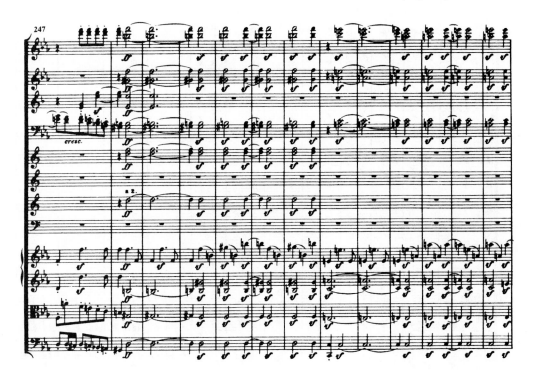

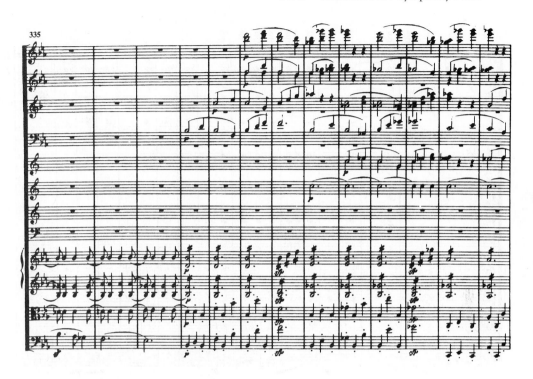

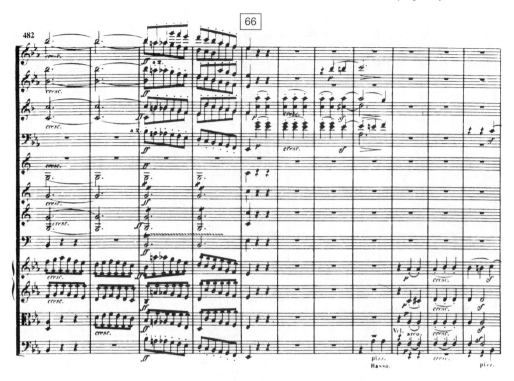

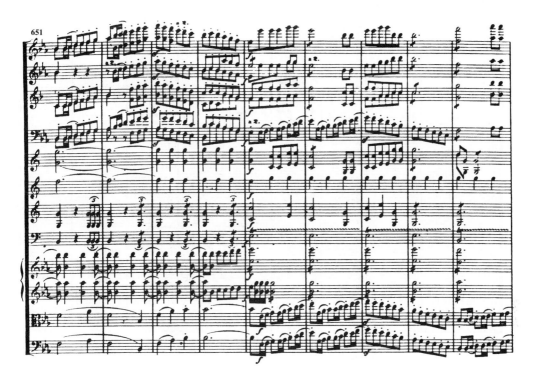

The Third Symphony was immediately recognized as an important work of unprecedented length and complexity. All the movements departed in unexpected ways from Beethoven's previous symphonic writing. Some of the unusual features can best be explained by reference to the purpose stated in the title of its first publication in 1806: "Heroic symphony . . . composed to celebrate the memory of a great man," ("Sinfonia Eroica . . . composta per festeggiare il sovvenire di un grand Uomo"). The first movement is particularly "heroic" in its expansive form, thematic richness, exciting climaxes, and forceful, obstinate assertion of individual imagination. Commentators and analysts as early as Beethoven's own time have pointed out certain peculiarities of the first movement.

1. The development section (245 measures) outweighs the exposition (155 measures) and recapitulation (154 measures), which are about equal. The coda (140 measures) is nearly as long as the exposition.
2. The bridge from the tonic group to the secondary or dominant thematic group is very short, while the latter has a multiplicity of themes.
3. A new theme is presented in the development.
4. There are disconcerting and abrupt changes of key, such as the succession E♭–F–D♭ within fifteen measures (measures 401–16) in the recapitulation, and E♭–D♭–C (measures 555–63) within eight measures of the coda.
5. Certain passages are insistently dissonant.
6. The French horn seems to state the main theme prematurely just before the recapitulation.

Points 2, 3, and 6 are debatable. Beethoven's early drafts give us some insight into his grand design and the function of these elements in it.

The question of the bridge and second theme section hinges on how we interpret the passages in measures 45–56 and 57–65. The first long "continuity draft" of the exposition contains just a suggestion of measures 45–56 (Example 1). This fragment is enough to help us identify the motive of measure 45 as growing out of the descending tail of the main theme (E♭–D–C♯, first heard in measures 6–7).

Example 1. Continuity draft from MS Landsberg 6, p. 11, after Nottebohm, *Ein Skizzenbuch von Beethoven aus dem Jahre 1803,* pp. 6–7, over outline of parallel passages in published score, measures 1–129

A revision to the above draft (Example 2, measures 45–56) elaborates on this idea for twelve measures and shows the modulatory passage of measures 57–65 almost fully formed. The passage has the character of Haydn's unstable, rushing, tutti transition sections and may have been intended to fulfill this function. The next passage, measures 65–83 of the final score, appears in this draft as a rhythmic variation on the sixteenth-note turns and leaping figures of measures 29–35. The entire section of this draft that later became measures 45–83 may be interpreted as a transition to and establishment of the dominant key, Bb.

Although one might gain the surface impression that Beethoven's final version abounds in new material, actually it draws motives from the first theme section, in keeping with past symphonic practice. As Beethoven worked with the material of his first drafts, the genesis of various components became obscured by imaginative spinoffs—namely, the three quite distinct motivic variants that make up the section from measure 45 to measure 83. A plausible conclusion is that this section is a bridge to the dominant-key section that begins at measure 83. Accordingly, three transitional motives may be identified: 1T at measure 45, 2T at measure 57, and 3T at measure 65. In this view, the bridge is of a length proportionate to the dimensions of the movement, and the second theme is a tonally stable and formal statement constructed of four-measure phrases. The entire texture of this theme participates in its exposition.

Example 2. Revision to the above draft of measures 45–56 from MS Landsberg 6, p. 10, after Nottebohm, pp. 8–9

Some have interpreted the passage from measures 45 to 56 as the first element of a multiple second theme group. Another view of this passage has it forming a bridge to the secondary theme section, which would be seen as arriving in the B♭-major passage at measure 57. This would assume a disproportionately short transition and a sly entry of the second theme group. Some analysts support this view even after seeing the sketches. It may be that Beethoven deliberately or unconsciously built into the exposition the ambiguity that stimulates these latter-day disagreements about details of the movement's form.

The issue of the "new theme" in the development has also occasioned much comment. Here again the drafts are enlightening. The so-called new theme in E minor played by the oboes at measure 284 does not appear at that point in any of the drafts. Instead we find a variant on the primary theme. Example 3 shows a relatively early draft, above the final version, and Example 4 shows how this variant derives from the corresponding notes of the main theme, transformed from major to minor. The *sfp* markings (*sforzando* followed by *piano*) on the notes G and B reinforce the identity of the main theme. At measure 292, where the key of A minor is reached, the draft gives a fragment of the counterpoint that was eventually given to the first oboe to accompany this variant of the main theme. What has been called the new theme is thus a counterpoint to a recall of the main theme.

Example 3. Continuity draft from MS Landsberg 6, pp. 38–39, over outline of parallel passages in published score

Example 4. "New theme"

Far from crowding the movement with a plethora of themes, Beethoven evidently kept very much to the elemental ideas announced in the first thirty-six measures. He preferred here the unitary motivic concentration of Haydn to the melodic abundance of Mozart.

What is new, however, is that the principal theme is treated like a character in a drama, portrayed as striving, being opposed and subdued but triumphing in the end. The entire symphony, indeed, acts out a drama, particularly the development section. At measure 186, the main theme contends with what we have called the third bridge motive (3T). At measure 220, the main theme in slow motion is subdued by its offspring, the first bridge motive (1T). This in turn becomes the subject of a short fugue, for which the countersubject is drawn from the third bridge motive.

The most dramatic event is the development of the syncopated, leaping outgrowth of the main theme that was first heard in measure 25; it culminates in the dissonances of measures 276–79, where an *E* suspended from a C-major chord is struck repeatedly over an F-chord, the Neapolitan chord of E minor. In this most remote key reached in the development section, the main theme appears crushed and subdued. It is heard against the counterpointing oboes, only to rise again through several metamorphoses. One of the most suggestive of these reappearances is at measure 394 in the French horn, when the theme tentatively rears its head against the solitary seventh and ninth of the dominant chord in the violins, just before the full orchestra sounds the complete dominant seventh to mark the arrival of the recapitulation. Early listeners

accused the horn of entering too soon; Carl Czerny, Beethoven's pupil, thought this entrance should be eliminated, and even Berlioz thought it was a copyist's mistake, but the sketches show that Beethoven contemplated this clever ploy from the very first drafts (see the autograph score, reproduced above).

The main points of arrival are indicated in the diagram below (the spacing is not proportional to time elapsed). Two possible interpretations of the thematic grouping are marked (1) and (2).

Section:	Intro.	Exposition						Development	Recapitulation						Coda	
Key:	E♭	→(B♭)		B♭				→	E♭							
Themes (1):		P	1T	2T	3T	S	K		P	1T	2T	3T	S	K		
Themes (2):		P	T	1S	2S	3S	K		P	T	1S	2S	3S	K		
Measures:	1	3	45	57	65	83	109 ‖:	152	398	448	460	468	486	512	551	691

LUDWIG VAN BEETHOVEN

String Quartet in C–sharp Minor, No. 14, Op. 131

First and second movements

a) Adagio ma non troppo e molto espressivo (first movement)

Complete String Quartets (New York: Dover, 1975), pp. 119–26.

b) Allegro molto vivace (second movement)

In 1826 Beethoven completed his Op. 131 quartet, one of five that he worked on in his last years. A subtle thematic connection and identity of key unite the first and last of its seven movements, which are played without pause. The slow first movement is a fugue on a subject made up of two segments, marked a and b in the example on the facing page. Only the first formal exposition engages all four voices; after that, statements of the subject in fragmentary form or in diminution are separated by episodes that develop motive a or b. The final section (measures 91–121) is a series of strettos, including a statement in the cello in augmentation (measure 99). All these devices are normal for a learned fugue.

What makes this fugue stand apart is its extreme emotionalism: the composer marked it "molto espressivo" and filled the score with precise indications of crescendos, sforzandos, rinforzandos, and diminuendos. Another unusual feature is the fugal answer in the subdominant rather than the dominant, and because it is a "real" answer (duplicating the intervals of the subject exactly), a conflict immediately arises between F♯ minor and the tonic C♯ minor. This conflict is resolved in favor of the tonic (measure 31), but then an enharmonic modulation to E♭ minor and another to G♯ minor cloud the horizon, until a hint at A major (measures 63–67) clears the air and assures a path back to C♯ minor. The movement ends with a sustained C♯-major chord, preparing for a slide from the single pitch *C♯* up to *D* to begin the next movement. This D-major goal may help to explain the answer in F♯ minor and the sforzandos on *A* in the subject and on *D* in the answer.

The second movement may be viewed as a contracted sonata form or simply as a ternary A B A form. It is based on a single theme, a folklike tune in ⁶⁄₈ first presented against a triple-drone that shifts between the tonic and subdominant. A bridge section (measure 24) develops a motive from this theme and leads to a short closing passage on C♯ major. A fermata marks the end of the expository section (measure 48). The middle section wends swiftly from C♯ minor back to D major for a reprise of the main theme in the viola (measure 84), with the drone now on the dominant note and shifted to the first violin. Continued development of this and the bridge motive culminates in a striking unison passage (measure 175–82). Significant in this movement, as in the first, is the use of *C♯* as a substitute dominant and the meticulously marked, sometimes abrupt changes in dynamics—and here also of tempo. In this movement Beethoven appears to have set aside formal repetitions and divisions and to have allowed one thought to lead to another as long as both pertained to the main theme.

108 HECTOR BERLIOZ (1803–1869)

Symphonie fantastique

III. *Scène aux champs;* IV. *Marche au supplice*

III [not included on recording]

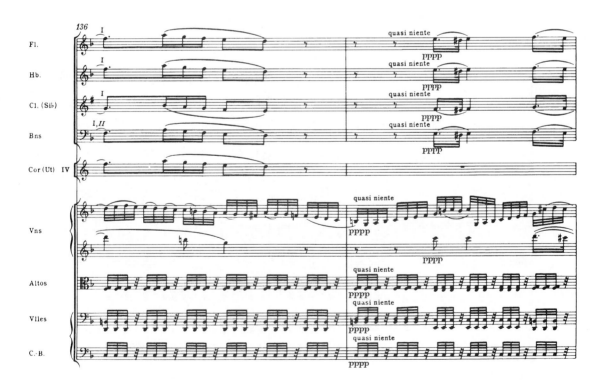

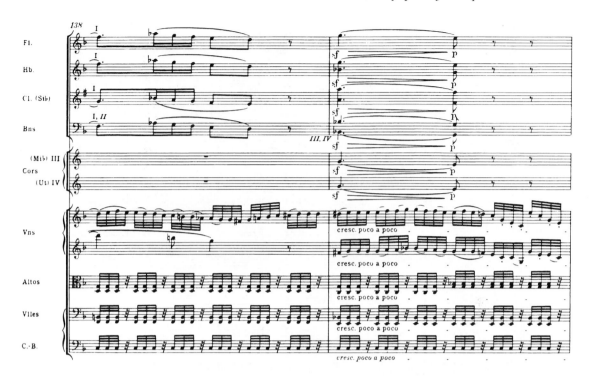

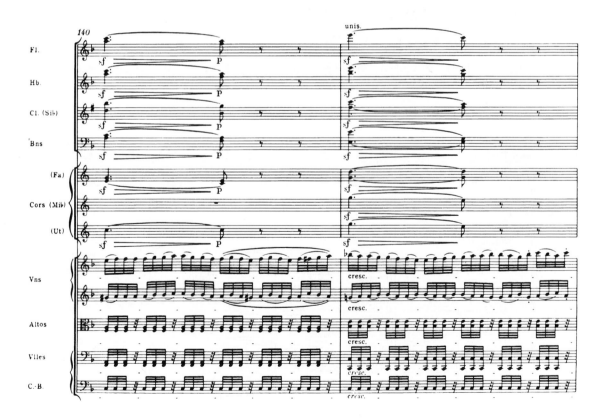

IV

Berlioz originally called this symphony "An Episode in the Life of an Artist, Fantastic Symphony in Five Parts." The first printed score of 1845 contained a detailed program, which the composer likened to the text of an opera. The first movement represents the passions of a young musician who sees for the first time in real life the woman of his dreams, an image that obsesses him, symbolized by a melody—an *idée fixe* (fixation; see the example below)—throughout the symphony.

In the second movement the artist finds himself at a ball, but the melody prevents him from enjoying the waltz. The next two scenes, given here in score, had the following program:

Program note distributed at first performance and published with the score in 1845:

AVERTISSEMENT	NOTE
Le Compositeur a eu pour but de développer, dans ce qu'elles ont de musical, différentes situations de la vie d'un artiste. Le plan du drame instrumental, privé du secours de la parole, a besoin d'être exposé d'avance. Le programme suivant doit donc être considéré comme le texte parlé d'un Opéra, servant à amener des morceaux de musique, dont il motive le caractère et l'expression.	The composer's intention has been to develop, insofar as they contain musical possibilities, various situations in the life of an artist. The outline of the instrumental drama, which lacks the help of words, needs to be explained in advance. The following program should thus be considered as the spoken text of an opera, serving to introduce the musical movements, whose character and expression it motivates.

[Précis of First and Second Parts: The author imagines that a young musician has fallen desperately in love with a woman who embodies all that he has imagined in his dreams. She is linked in his mind with a melody, so that the melody and the model become a double *idée fixe,* which reappears in every movement of the symphony. The passage from melancholic reverie to frenzied passion, jealousy, and tenderness is the subject of the first movement. In the second the artist finds himself at a ball, where the beloved image appears and disturbs his peace of mind.]

TROISIÈME PARTIE
Scène aux champs
Se trouvant un soir à la campagne, il entend au loin deux pâtres qui dialoguent un ranz de vaches; ce duo pastoral, le lieu de la scène, le léger bruissement des arbres doucement agités par le vent, quelques motifs d'espérance qu'il a conçus depuis peu, tout concourt à rendre à son coeur un calme inaccoutumé, et à donner à ses idées une couleur plus riante. Il réfléchit sur son isolement; il espère n'être bientôt plus seul . . . . Mais si elle le trompait! . . . Ce mélange d'espoir et de crainte, ces idées de bonheur troublées par quelques noirs pressentiments, forment le sujet de l'ADAGIO. A la fin, l'un des pâtres reprend le ranz de vaches; l'autre ne répond plus . . . Bruit éloigné de tonnerre . . . solitude . . . silence . . . .

THIRD PART
Scene in the Country
Finding himself one evening in the country, he hears in the distance two shepherds piping a *ranz de vaches* in dialogue. This pastoral duet, the scenery, the quiet rustling of the trees gently brushed by the wind, the hopes he has recently found some reason to entertain —all concur in affording his heart an unaccustomed calm, and in giving a more cheerful color to his ideas. He reflects upon his isolation; he hopes that his loneliness will soon be over.— But what if she were deceiving him!—The mingling of hope and fear, these ideas of happiness disturbed by black presentiments, form the subject of the Adagio. At the end one of the shepherds again takes up the *ranz de vaches;* the other no longer replies.— Distant sound of thunder— loneliness—silence.

QUATRIÈME PARTIE
Marche au supplice
Ayant acquis la certitude que son amour est méconnu, l'artiste s'empoisonne avec de l'opium. La dose du narcotique, trop faible pour lui donner la mort, le plonge dans un sommeil accompagné de plus horribles visions. Il rêve qu'il a tué celle qu'il aimait, qu'il est condamné, conduit au supplice, et qu'il assiste à sa PROPRE EXECUTION. Le cortège s'avance aux sons d'une marche tantôt sombre et farouche, tantôt brillante et solennelle, dans laquelle un bruit sourd de pas graves succède sans transition aux éclats les plus bruyants. A la fin de la marche, les quatre premières mésures de l'IDÉE FIXE reparaissent comme une dernière pensée d'amour interrompue par le coup fatal.

FOURTH PART
March to the Scaffold
Convinced that his love is unappreciated, the artist poisons himself with opium. The dose of the narcotic, too weak to kill him, plunges him into a sleep accompanied by the most horrible visions. He dreams that he has killed his beloved, that he is condemned and led to the scaffold, and that he is witnessing *his own execution.* The procession moves forward to the sounds of a march that is now sombre and fierce, now brilliant and solemn, in which the muffled noise of heavy steps gives way without transition to the noisiest clamor. At the end of the march the first four measures of the *idée fixe* reappear, like a last thought of love interrupted by the fatal blow.
—Translated by Edward T. Cone

The *Scene in the Country* opens with a duet of pipers that pays tribute to Beethoven's *Pastoral* Symphony, which Berlioz so much admired. Beethoven had begun his fifth movement with a dialogue between the clarinet and French horn; Berlioz began with an oboe and English horn behind the scenes, and the music is that of a Swiss cowherd's call *(ranz de vaches)*. As in

Beethoven, there are also bird calls (measures 67–71). Another gesture derived from Beethoven—this time the Ninth Symphony—is the sudden appearance of a recitative (measure 87) in the bassoons, cellos, and double basses, now answered by successive fragments of the *idée fixe* in the flutes and oboes, as the artist—the hero of the *Fantastic* Symphony—recalls the woman of his dreams. Another Beethovenian touch is the breaking up of the cowherd's call at the end of the movement, just as Beethoven had broken up the main theme at the end of the Funeral March of the *Eroica* Symphony.

The *March to the Scaffold,* on the other hand, is full of unprecedented orchestral effects. Berlioz had originally conceived this march for the opera *Les Francs-juges.* The opening timpani duet in minor thirds, accompanied by French horns stopped with the hand rather than valves, and double basses playing pizzicato in four-part harmony paint the eerie picture of an execution, to which the hero of Berlioz's drama is being led. Another novelty is a theme in the double basses and cellos that descends the melodic-minor scale, marked by a foreboding rhythm (measure 17). The main march theme in the relative major (measure 62), is a fanfare based on the open notes of the horn, doubled by all the winds of the orchestra, including two ophicleides (keyed bass bugles). Realistic touches include the loud tutti chord that follows the quotation of the *idée fixe* at measure 164, representing the drop of the guillotine's blade, and the softer descent in the pizzicato strings indicating the fall of the head, after which the crowd is heard cheering above the sound of muffled drums and three timpani rolling a major chord.

Felix Mendelssohn (1809–1847)
Incidental Music to *A Midsummer Night's Dream,* Op. 61

Scherzo 　7

Mendelssohn, *Musik zu Sommernachtstraum von Shakespeare* (Leipzig: Breitkopf & Härtel, 1874–77; repr. New York: Dover, 1975), pp. 55–71.

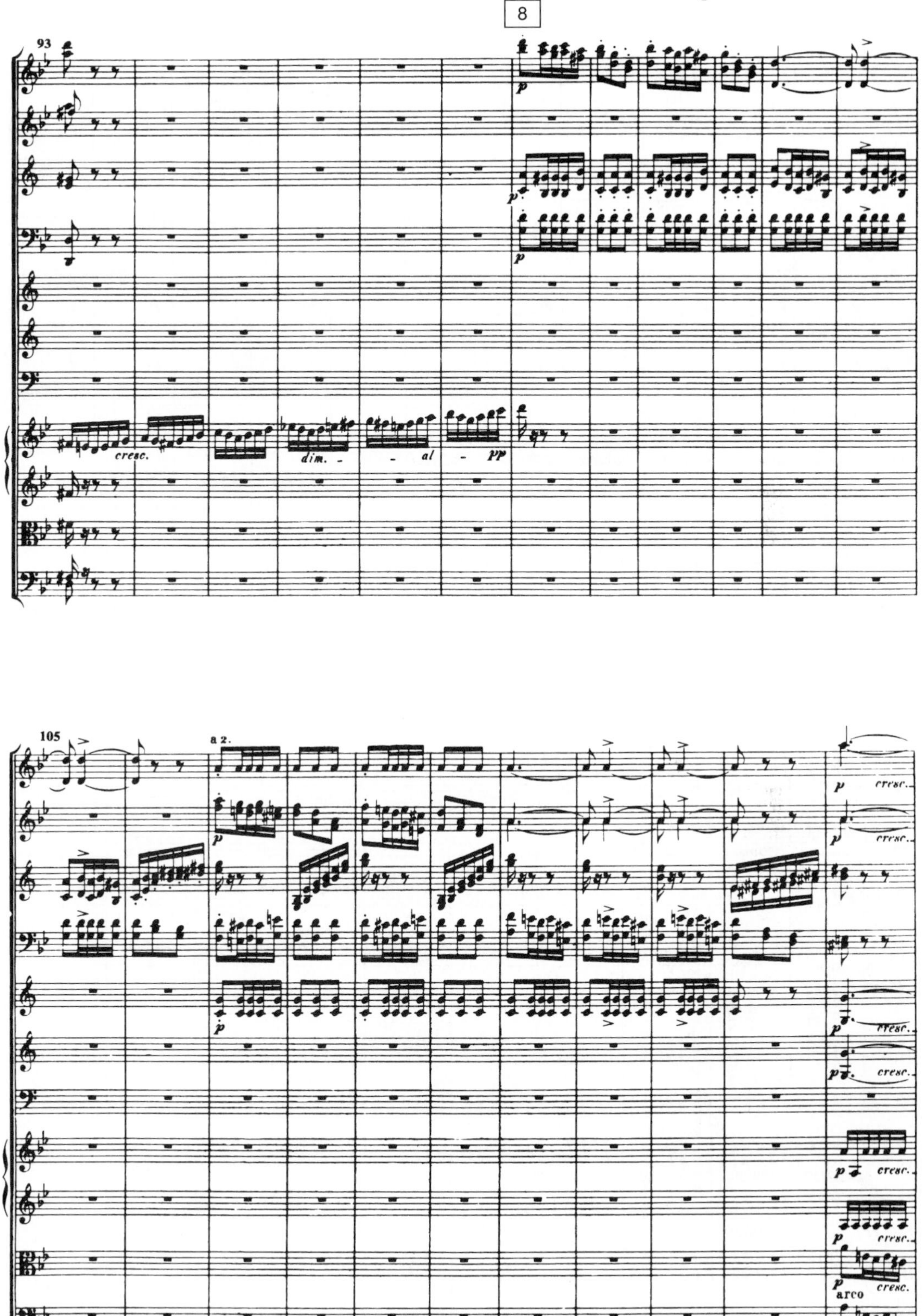
8
93
cresc.
dim. - - al - pp
105
a 2.
arco
cresc.

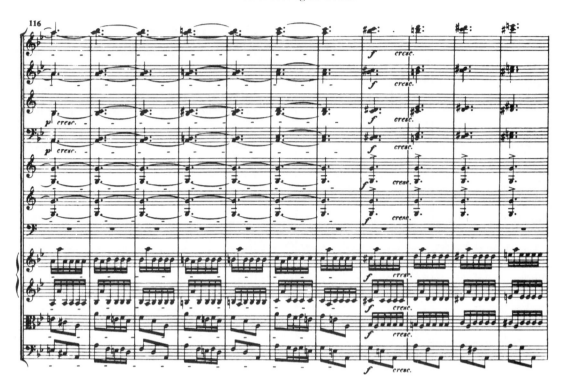

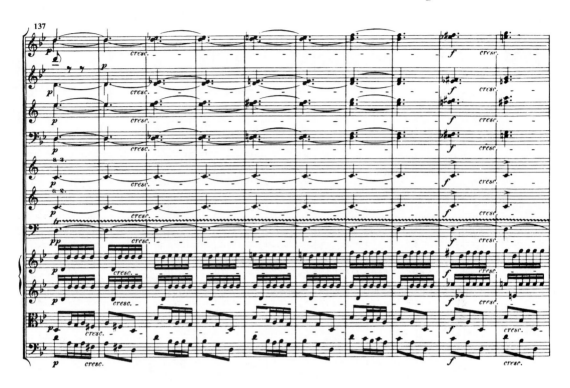

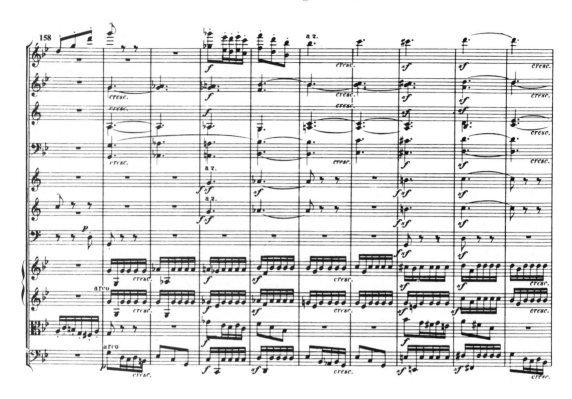

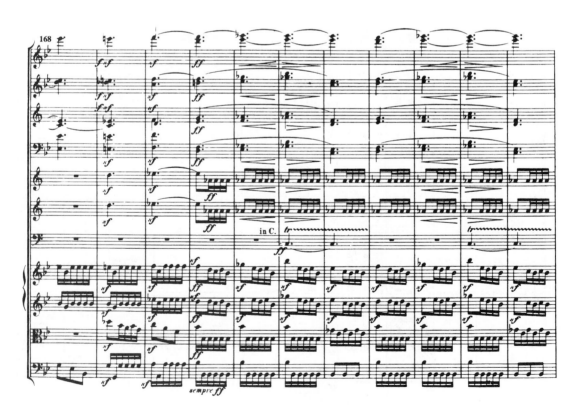

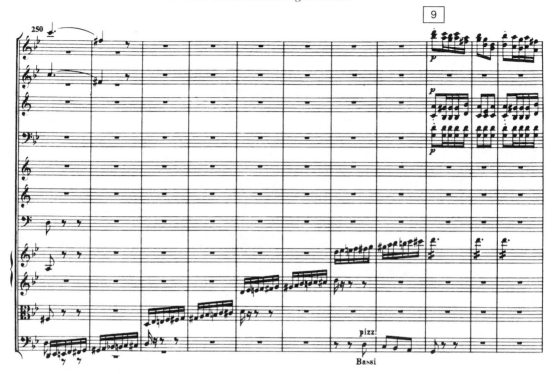

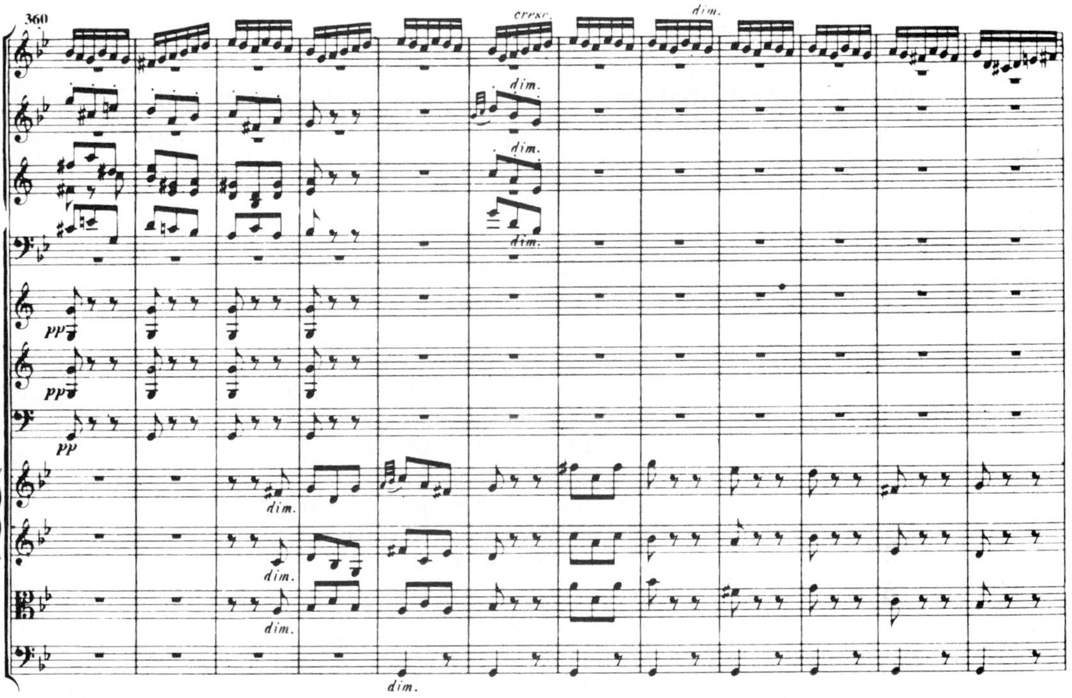
360
cresc.
dim.
pp

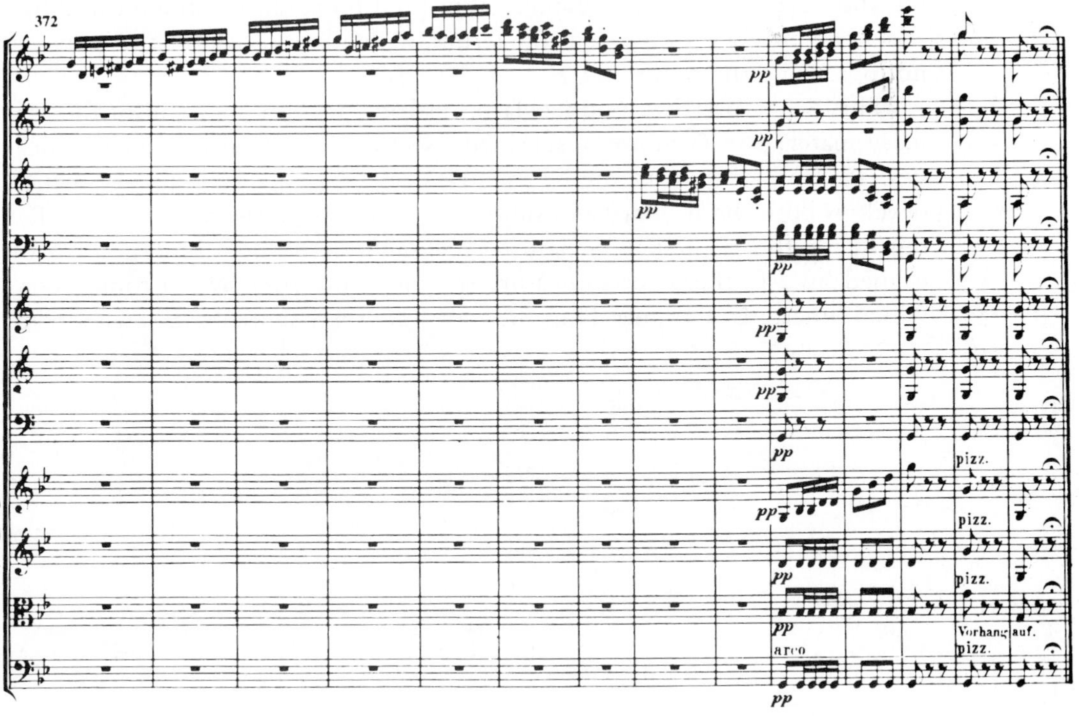
372
pp
pizz.
Vorhang auf.
arco

Intended to be played before the second act of Shakespeare's play, this music is a brilliant example of self-renewing perpetual motion and of a heavy orchestra tamed to tiptoe like a chamber ensemble. It leads into the Fairy's speech at the beginning of Act II:

> Over hill, over dale,
> Through bush, through brier,
> Over park, over pale,
> Through flood, through fire,
> I do wander every where,
> Swifter than the moon's sphere;
> And I serve the fairy Queen,
> To dew her orbs upon the green.
> The cowslips tall her pensioners be;
> In their gold coats spots you see;
> Those be rubies, fairy favours,
> In those freckles live their savours.

Seventeen years earlier Mendelssohn had written an overture to the play and in 1843 wrote additional music, which included this picturesque Scherzo. Although it may be called programmatic (in the same sense as Beethoven's *Pastoral* Symphony) and is certainly Romantic in the quality of its imagination and its treatment of the orchestra, it avoids extremes of feeling and never allows the extramusical inspiration to disturb the musical balance. The program thinly veils the structure, lending charm to the view but not obscuring the outlines.

This Scherzo lacks the usual Trio. Instead, after presentation of the primary material in G minor, a subsidiary section in the relative major (measure 48), and a return to the first material, an extended modulatory section develops both the primary and subsidiary material (measures 129–258). The reprise in the main key (measures 258–338) is full of fresh new turns, capped by a feathery forty-measure staccato flute solo over a tonic pedal, which functions as a coda. Thus the movement is essentially in sonata form.

ROBERT SCHUMANN (1810–1856)

Phantasiestücke, Op. 12

Nos. 4 and 5

a) No. 4: *Grillen*

b) No. 5: *In der Nacht*

Schumann himself gave the eight pieces of the *Phantasiestücke* their whimsi-cal titles, and the element binding them together is the free flight of imagi-nation they display. *Grillen* (Whims) is typical of Schumann's approach to composition in the late 1830s. It is built entirely of four-measure phrases that join to form five distinct musical periods or modules, which recur in the rondo-like pattern A B C B A D E A B C B A:

Section:	A	B	C	B	A	D	E	A	B	C	B	A
Tonal center:	D♭	f	A♭	f	D♭	G♭		D♭	b♭	D♭	b♭	D♭
Measure:	1	17	25	37	45	61	73	96	113	121	133	141	156

Although the periods are subtly linked through rhythmic, melodic, and har-monic motives, they are essentially independent blocks of music. When they recur, they remain intact and unvaried (aside from transposition) and can be joined front to back or back to front—that is, A may proceed to B, or B to A, and similarly with C and B. Like most short pieces of Schumann, *Grillen* has a triple-time dance flavor, in which the middle section (DE) functions as a trio. The fantastic element is particularly felt in the tonal organization. Although the opening suggests B♭ minor, the only cadences in the first period are on A♭ and D♭, in which the first period ends. The B and C sections fluctuate less ambiguously between A♭ major and F minor, while the trio is clearly in G♭ major.

The *Phantasiestücke* were written in 1837 when Schumann was courting his bride-to-be Clara Wieck, then a girl of eighteen. But he was in Leipzig and she in Vienna or touring as a concert pianist. Her father objected to the relationship but allowed Clara to correspond with Robert. *In der Nacht* (In the Night), Schumann admitted, made him think wistfully of crossing the chasm that separated them, like the legendary Hero and Leander. He wrote to Clara about it:

> You know the story well. Every night Leander swims across the sea to his beloved, who waits in the lighthouse and shows him the way with a torch. It is a nice old romantic saga. When I play *In der Nacht* I cannot get the scene out of my mind— first, how he plunges into the sea; she calls, he answers; how he gets through the waves and reaches land—now comes the cantabile, as they hold each other in their arms—how, then, he must set forth again but cannot tear himself away, until night again envelops everything in darkness.[*]

This was the image that Schumann's own fantasy wove around music that he had already written. It is not a program, but it recognizes a narrative design in the music. Schumann did not relate how the legend ends: one night a storm snuffs out the guiding light, Leander founders in the heavy seas, Hero jumps in to save him, and both drown.

Marked "Mit Leidenschaft" (with passion), the piece has a persistent sixteenth-note motion in $\frac{2}{4}$, a true *moto perpetuo*. An almost constant broken-chord figure serves as a background to a descending-second motive and brief melodic eruptions in triplets. Unprepared lower neighbors (for example, the G♯ in measure 5, the F♯ in measure 6) disturb the smooth surface of the broken chords. The large form is ternary, with a fast main section in F minor and a slightly slower lyrical middle section in F major. In the *cantabile* middle section (the couple's embrace in Schumann's letter) the triplet melody of the first section intrudes twice in the low register, and a whirring, accelerating transition that temporarily abandons the broken-chord figure seems almost to describe a stormy sea.

---

[*]Letter, April 21, 1838, Robert Schumann to Clara Wieck; original German text in *Clara und Robert Schumann, Briefwechsel, Kritische Gesamtausgabe*, ed. Eva Weissweibe, Vol. 1 (Stroemfeld: Roter Stern, 1984), p. 154.

111 JOHN FIELD (1782–1837)
Nocturne in A Major, No. 8

This composition first published in a longer version (96 measures) as a *Pastorale* in the *Second Divertimento for Piano with Accompaniment of a String Quartet* (Moscow, *ca.* 1811; London, *ca.* 1811–12). In 1815 it appeared in the present version as the first of three *Romances for Piano* (Leipzig, 1815), eventually becoming one of the *Nocturnes,* usually called No. 8, but actually No. 9 (see Cecil Hopkinson, *A Bibliographical Thematic Catalogue of the Works of John Field,* London, 1961, p. 33). Reprinted from *Nocturnes,* rev. by Louis Koehler (Frankfurt, etc., Peters n.d., pl. no. 6515), pp. 28–31.

Field's Nocturne No. 8 (published 1801) exhibits a number of parallels to Chopin's Op. 9, No. 2 (1830–31; see No. 112, on following pages), particularly the rising major sixth, the soulful turn, and the chromatic ornamentation of the melody against a barcarolle accompaniment. The embellishment of Field's line (compare measures 18–24 with 25–32) emulates the ornamentation and cadenzas practiced by operatic singers and taken over by pianists in their improvised variations on favorite arias, many of which have come down to us as published pieces. Although Field anticipated some of Chopin's mannerisms, he could not match the rich harmonic imagination that so powerfully supports Chopin's lyrical lines, as in the E-flat Nocturne.

Fryderyk Chopin (1810–1849)

Nocturne in E-flat Major, Op. 9, No. 2

Reprinted from *Nocturnes*, rev. by Hermann Scholtz (Frankfurt: Peters, n.d., pl. no. 9026), pp. 8–10.

113 FRANZ LISZT (1811–1886)

Nuages gris

Reprinted from *Late Piano Works,* Vol. I, pp. 15–16, © copyright 1952 by Schott & Co., Ltd., London. Used by permission of European American Music Distributors Corp. Sole U.S. Agent for Schott & Co., London.

In this late work of Liszt (Gray Clouds, 1881), the most prominent chord is the augmented triad of measure 11, *Bb-D-F#*. From it Liszt slides down by half steps until he reaches an inversion of the same chord in measure 19, *D-F#-Bb,* likewise an augmented triad. This progression is accompanied by a *tremolando* descending-semitone ostinato *Bb–A*.

When the passage is recapitulated at the end in the left hand (measures 35–42), it stops short of the goal, on the augmented chord *Eb-G-Cb*. Now the parallel series of augmented chords descending by semitone is heard in a broken texture accompanying a slowly rising melody in octaves through fourteen steps of the chromatic scale, culminating at *g'''*. The tonal center *G* is affirmed at the final cadence chiefly by slowing down the movement and the full-measure pause before the appoggiatura–like *F#–G* in the melody. Meanwhile the last augmented chord heard, *Eb-G-Cb,* continues to be reiterated until the end over the last note of the ostinato, *A,* never to be resolved.* In works such as this, Liszt in the last fifteen years of his life ventured into uncharted territory of harmonic and contrapuntal practice.

*For an analysis of this work from the standpoint of voice-leading and pitch-class sets, as well as a bibliography of other analytical studies which consider it from various points of view, see Allen Forte, "Liszt's Experimental Idiom and Music of the Early Twentieth Century," *19th Century Music* 10 (1987):209–28.

JOHANNES BRAHMS (1833–1897)
Piano Quintet in F Minor, Op. 34

Scherzo (third movement)

Reprinted from Edition Eulenburg, 1954, pp. 35–47.

Brahms had already crystallized his personal idiom in this early work (1864). The opening of this movement has been compared to that of Beethoven's Scherzo in the Fifth Symphony. But Beethoven clearly spelled out C minor, while Brahms clouded the tonal feeling by spreading the Ab-major melody over an insistent C pedal. The ambiguity is not cleared up until the broadly spanned soaring theme has unfolded in the first violin and reaches the dominant of C minor (measure 13). Brahms's humor relies on a quick repartee: shifts between $\frac{6}{8}$ and $\frac{2}{4}$, and between *fortissimo* homorhythms and hushed cross-rhythms and syncopations. Besides these contrasts, the Scherzo exploits the harmonic colors of a broad spectrum of keys, relating both to C minor and C major. Striking is the use of the Neapolitan chord as a kind of dominant in the cadential passage just before the Trio.

The Trio, like Beethoven's, is in C major. Where Beethoven invented truly contrasting material and textures, Brahms developed the same ideas as in the Scherzo. The entire movement's robust rhythms and the fleeting hints of a hurdy-gurdy in its persistent pedal points give it an earthy quality true to the Beethovenian tradition.

Franz Schubert (1797–1828)

Gretchen am Spinnrade, D. 118

Reprinted from Breitkopf & Härtel Critical Edition of 1884–97, Series 20, 1:191–96.

Meine Ruh' ist hin,
Mein Herz ist schwer;
Ich finde sie nimmer
Und nimmermehr.

Wo ich ihn nicht hab'
Ist mir das Grab,
Die ganze Welt
Ist mir vergällt.

Mein armer Kopf
Ist mir verrückt,
Mein armer Sinn
Ist mir zerstückt.

Meine Ruh' ist hin,
Mein Herz ist schwer;
Ich finde sie nimmer
Und nimmermehr.

Nach ihm nur schau' ich
Zum Fenster hinaus,
Nach ihm nur geh' ich
Aus dem Haus.

Sein hoher Gang,
Sein' edle Gestalt,
Seines Mundes Lächeln,
Seiner Augen Gewalt,

Und seiner Rede
Zauberfluß,
Sein Händedruck,
Und, ach, sein Kuß!

Meine Ruh' ist hin,
Mein Herz ist schwer;
Ich finde sie nimmer
Und nimmermehr.

Mein Busen drängt sich
Nach ihm hin;
Ach, dürft' ich fassen
Und halten ihn

Und küssen ihn,
So wie ich wollt',
An seinen Küssen
Vergehen sollt'!

Meine Ruh' ist hin.

—JOHANN WOLFGANG VON GOETHE
From *Faust,* Part 1

My peace is gone.
My heart is heavy.
I'll never find peace,
ever again.

Where he's not with me
it's like a tomb,
the world around
a bitter place.

My poor head
is turned upside down.
My poor senses
are torn apart.

My peace is gone.
My heart is heavy.
I'll never find peace,
ever again.

For him only, I look
out the window.
For him only, I go
out of the house.

His lofty bearing,
his noble air,
the smile on his lips,
the strength of his gaze,

his talk's
magic flow,
the touch of his hand,
and, ah, his kiss!

My peace is gone.
My heart is heavy.
I'll never find peace,
ever again.

My heart pines
for him.
Ah, if I could touch him
and hold him

and kiss him
all I wanted,
in his kisses
I would be lost.

My peace is gone.

Gretchen am Spinnrade (Gretchen at the Spinning Wheel) is one of Schubert's most famous lieder. Already in this early work (1814), the accompaniment claims a large share of the listener's attention. The piano part suggests not only the whirr of the spinning wheel by a constant sixteenth-note figure in the right hand and the motion of the treadle by the repeated rhythmic pattern in the left hand, but also the agitation of Gretchen's thoughts, her peace gone, as she thinks of her beloved in Goethe's epic poem *Faust*. The restlessness is also reflected in the harmony, in the tension between D minor and C major and suggestions of C minor in the opening stanza. The second and third stanzas (measures 13–29) flirt with E major, E minor, and F major.

Schubert's obvious desire to maintain constant motion and renewal ruled out the purely strophic setting that was common in lieder at this time. In the midst of change, both the poem and the composition gain shape, unity, and stability by the return of the first stanza and its music as the fourth and eighth, dividing the song into three parts.

When, in the sixth and seventh stanzas (measures 50–67), Gretchen extols her idol's qualities, the harmony reaches for A♭ major, and the singer strains for the highest note so far, on the words "and, ah, his kiss," stopping on a diminished-seventh chord (measure 68). The piano now lingers for a short interlude on the dominant harmony, mostly avoided up to now, in preparation for the last return of the opening music. After the final stanza, Schubert drew freely from the poem to create a coda (measures 100–20), which emphasizes with the highest notes of the song Gretchen's fantasy of being lost in her lover's kisses—"an seinen Küssen vergehen sollt'."

116 FRANZ SCHUBERT

Winterreise, D. 911

Der Lindenbaum

Reprinted from Breitkopf & Härtel Critical Edition of 1884–97, Series 20, Vol. 9.

32

Ich musst' auch heu_te wan_dern vor_bei in tie_fer Nacht, da

hab ich noch im Dun_kel die Au gen zu_ge_macht. Und sei_ ne Zweige

rausch_ten, als rie _ fen sie mir zu: komm her zu mir, Ge_sel_le, hier

33

find'st ____ du dei_ne Ruh! Die

kal _ ten Win_de blie _ sen mir grad' in's An _ ge_

Am Brunnen vor dem Thore
Da steht ein Lindenbaum;
Ich träumt' in seinem Schatten
So manchen süssen Traum.

Ich schnitt in seine Rinde
So manches liebe Wort;
Es zog in Freud' und Leide
Zu ihm mich immer fort.

Ich musst' auch heute wandern
Vorbei in tiefer Nacht,
Da hab' ich noch im Dunkel
Die Augen zugemacht.

Und seine Zweige rauschten,
Als riefen sie mir zu:
Komm her zu mir, Geselle,
Hier find'st du deine Ruh!

Die kalten Winde bließen
Mir grad' in's Angesicht,
Der Hut flog mir von Kopfe,
Ich wendete mich nicht.

Nun bin ich manche Stunde
Entfernt von jenem Ort,
Und immer hör' ich's rauschen:
Du fändest Ruhe dort!

   —WILHELM MÜLLER

At the well by the gate
stands a linden tree.
I dreamt in its shade
many a sweet dream.

I carved into its bark
many a word of love.
In joy and sorrow
I was always drawn to it.

Again today I had to walk
by it in the deep of night,
even in the dark
I closed my eyes.

And its boughs rustled
as if calling to me:
"Come to me, companion,
here you'll find your rest."

The cold winds blew
straight into my face.
My hat flew off my head,
I did not turn around.

Now I am some hours
away from that place,
and always I hear it rustle:
"You would find your rest there."

The song cycle *Winterreise* (Winter's Journey, 1827) consists of twenty-four poems by Wilhelm Müller that express the nostalgia of a lover revisiting in winter the haunts of a failed summer romance. In *Der Lindenbaum* (The Linden Tree), the poet dwells on the memory of the tree under which he used to lie dreaming of his love. Now, as he passes it, the icy wind rustles the branches, which seem to call him back to find rest there once again.

Schubert borrowed the motive in the piano that accompanies the words "The cold winds blew" to set the stage with a seven-measure introduction, turning the music from the chilly minor to a sunnier major to evoke the happier mood of the summer. This music serves also for interludes and an epilogue. The song itself is in a modified strophic form, each strophe of music setting two stanzas of the poem. The first two stanzas are set to a simple, folklike melody made up of four-measure phrases in the form a abb′ and accompanied by simple chords. The next two stanzas repeat this melody but with a broken-chord accompaniment. The fifth stanza departs from the pattern to portray the blustery winter scene. The last stanza is sung twice to the music of the opening stanzas. Thus the overall form of the song is A A′ B A″.

Robert Schumann

Dichterliebe, Op. 48

Nos. 1 and 7

a) No. 1: *Im wunderschönen Monat Mai*

Reprinted from C. F. Peters Edition, Leipzig.

Im wunderschönen Monat Mai,
Als alle Knospen sprangen,
Da ist in meinem Herzen
Die Liebe aufgegangen.

In wunderschönen Monat Mai,
Als alle Vögel sangen,
Da hab' ich ihr gestanden
Mein Sehnen und Verlangen.

—HEINRICH HEINE

In the marvelous month of May,
when all the buds burst open,
then in my heart
love broke out.

In the marvelous month of May,
as all the birds sang,
then I confessed to her
my longing and desire.

b) No. 7: *Ich grolle nicht*

Ich grolle nicht und wenn das Herz auch bricht	I bear no grudge; even though my heart breaks,
Ewig verlor'nes Lieb, ich grolle nicht.	my forever lost love, I bear no grudge.
Wie du auch strahlst in Diamantenpracht,	Though you are radiant in your splendid diamonds,
Es fällt kein Strahl in deines Herzens Nacht.	no ray of light penetrates your heart's night.
Das weiss ich längst. Ich sah dich ja im Traume,	This have I long known. I saw you in a dream,
Und sah die Nacht in deines Herzens Raume,	and I saw the darkness in your heart's hollow
Und sah die Schlang', die dir am Herzen frisst,	and saw the serpent that feeds upon your heart.
Ich sah, mein Lieb, wie sehr du elend bist.	I saw, my love, how very pitiful you are.

—HEINRICH HEINE

The cycle *Dichterliebe* (A Poet's Love) consists of sixteen songs on poems selected from the more than sixty in Heinrich Heine's *Lyrisches Intermezzo* (1823 and later editions). The poems of the two songs presented here were first published in Heine's *Minnelieder* (1822). Neither Heine's collection nor Schumann's cycle has an encompassing narrative, but the theme of unrequited love prevails.

The first song of the cycle, *Im wunderschönen Monat Mai,* speaks happily of springtime and a newly confessed love, but the tonal ambiguity and tension between voice and piano may reflect the pessimistic outlook of the cycle as a whole. While the voice part seems to be in A major, in the second and last measures and strategic points along the way, including the very end, we hear the dominant-seventh chord of F♯ minor in the piano. The appoggiaturas and suspensions that begin almost every other measure, which Schumann added only in the final draft, betray the bittersweet anxiety of the lover. A clever link between voice and accompaniment is the anticipation of the descending-sixth figure in the first phrase of the voice by a similar ascending-sixth figure in the piano.

The two stanzas are set strophically. The four-measure piano prelude and postlude are characteristic of the songs in this cycle.

Schumann took some liberties with the text in the modified strophic setting of *Ich grolle nicht.* He borrowed a half line from the second stanza to end the first strophe so that he could tack on to the beginnning of the second the words "Ich grolle nicht," which thus function as a refrain. He also added two more repetitions of these words at the end of the song. Schumann's insistence on this thought brings out the irony of the poem, which states that the lover feels more pity than anger for the woman who has spurned him; yet the music is decidedly indignant, with its grating major sevenths and obstinately repeated chords.

CLARA WIECK SCHUMANN (1819–1896)

Geheimes Flüstern hier und dort, Op. 23, No. 3

From *Sechs Lieder aus Jucunde von Hermann Rollet[t] für eine Singstimme mit Begleitung des Pianoforte,* Op. 23, 1856, Joachim Draheim and Brigitte Höft, eds. In Clara Schumann, *Sämtliche Lieder für Singstimme und Klavier* (Wiesbaden: Breitkopf & Härtel, 1990), 1:40–41.

Geheimes Flüstern hier und dort,
Verborg'nes Quellenrauschen,
O Wald, o Wald, geweihter Ort,
Laß mich des Lebens reinstes Wort
In Zweig und Blatt belauschen!

Secret whispers here and there,
hidden rushing springs,
O woods, O woods, consecrated place,
allow me to listen to life's purest word
in the rustling of bough and leaf.

Und schreit' ich in den Wald hinaus,	And I stride out into the woods,
Da grüßen mich die Bäume,	where the trees greet me.
Du liebes, freies Gotteshaus,	You dear free house of God,
Du schließest mich mit Sturmgebraus	you shut me with the storm's roar
In deine kühlen Räume!	in your cool chambers.
Was leise mich umschwebt, umklingt,	What softly hovers and rings around me,
Ich will es treu bewahren,	I will faithfully treasure,
Und was mir tief zum Herzen dringt,	and what touches me deep in the heart
Will ich, vom Geist der Lieb' beschwingt,	will I, impelled by the spirit of Love,
Im Liedern offenbaren!	reveal in songs.

—HERMANN ROLLETT

This is one of six songs that Clara Schumann composed in 1853 on poems from the cycle *Jucunde* by Hermann Rollett (1819–1904). The uniform mood of the three stanzas, dominated by the image of the forest whispering to the poet, permits the strictly strophic setting. The perpetual sixteenth-note broken-chord motion in $\frac{3}{8}$ sets up a backdrop of rustling leaves and branches for the expression of the poet's dependence on the forest for refuge and as a communicator of life's secrets. But there remains the unresolved passion that, as the last lines say, can only be revealed in song.

The serenity of the prelude, interludes, and postlude is disturbed by the long appoggiaturas on the first beat of almost every other bar, representing the intense feelings that break into the calm of the woods. In a poignant touch, the unresolved G♭ in the voice in measure 32 is cut off and then resolved in the accompaniment, as the climactic thought of each stanza is reached on the words "reinstes Wort" (purest word), "Sturmgebraus" (the storm's roar), and "Geist der Lieb' beschwingt" (impelled by love). The one clear modulation is to F major (measure 23), the favored third-relation of the Romantic period.

119 ANTON BRUCKNER (1824–1896)

Virga Jesse

38

Alla breve

Bruckner, *Virga Jesse* (New York: Peters, 1961). Reprinted by permission.

Virga Jesse floruit	The rod of Jesse blossomed:
Virgo Deum et hominem genuit:	a virgin brought forth God and man;
pacem Deus reddidit,	peace God restored,
in se reconcilians ima summis.	in himself reconciling the lowest with the highest.
Alleluja.	Alleluia.

Bruckner composed this a cappella motet in 1885 in a modernized *stile anti-co*. The deceptively simple diatonic lines sung by the individual voices produce textures, harmonies, and modulations that are full of surprises and that anticipate twentieth-century choral writing. Yet the counterpoint is impeccable in its handling of dissonances and part-movement. Based in the tonality of E, the motet modulates through a series of steps marked by *Generalpausen* to G major and minor, B♭ major, G major, C minor, and back to E major.

GIOACHINO ROSSINI (1792–1868)

Il barbiere di Siviglia

Act II, Scene 5: *Una voce poco fa*

From the piano-vocal score (Milan: Ricordi, n.d.), pp. 102–09, based on the critical edition of the orchestral score (1969). Reprinted by permission.

cabaletta

ROSINA

Una voce poco fa	A voice a short while ago
Qui nel cor mi risuonò.	here in my heart resounded.
Il mio cor ferito è già,	My heart is already wounded,
E Lindor fu che il piagò.	and Lindoro is the culprit.
Sì, Lindoro mio sarà,	Yes, Lindoro will be mine.
Lo giurai la vincerò	I swore that I would win.
Il tutor ricuserò,	The guardian I shall refuse.
Io l'ingegno aguzzerò.	I shall sharpen my wits.
Alla fin s'accheterà,	In the end he will be appeased,
E contenta io resterò.	and I shall be happy.
Sì, Lindoro mio sarà . . .	Yes, Lindoro will be mine . . .
Io sono docile, son rispettosa,	I am docile, I am respectful,
Sono obbediente, dolce amorosa,	I am obedient, sweetly loving;
Mi lascio reggere, mi fo guidar.	I let myself be governed, to be led.
Ma se mi toccano dov'è il mio debole,	But if they touch my weaker side,
Sarò una vipera, e cento trappole	I can be a viper, and a hundred tricks
Prima di cedere farò giocar!	I'll play before I give in!

—Libretto by CESARE STERBINI
   after BEAUMARCHAIS

Il barbiere di Siviglia, on a libretto by Cesare Sterbini, based on Beaumarchais's *Le barbier de Séville,* was first performed in Rome on February 20, 1816.

   In this scene, Rosina recalls being serenaded by Count Almaviva posing as Lindoro, a poor romantic suitor. She resolves in the Andante section to win him; then in a Moderato she boasts that she can be docile and easy to manage until she is crossed, when she stings like a viper. The Andante, sometimes called a *cavatina* because its style is drawn *(cavato)* from that of recitative, in this case displays the wide leaps, parlando repeated notes, and cascading runs of obbligato recitative in the voice, punctuated by chords in the orchestra. When she speaks of getting rid of her old guardian, Dr. Bartolo, who wants to marry her, the violins wink at her with grace notes. The Moderato is a bravura aria, but its coloratura is restrained and contained within a regular periodicity that adds to its charm.

   When Rosina, after boasting that she has a hundred tricks—"cento trappole"—that she can play, returns to speak of being docile, the entire orchestra seems to join in her conspiracy.

121 VINCENZO BELLINI (1801–1835)

Norma

Act I, Scene 4: *Casta Diva*

From *Norma* (Milan: Ricordi, 1974), pp. 61–85. Reprinted by permission.

sempre cresc. sino al.....

sempre cresc. sino al..........

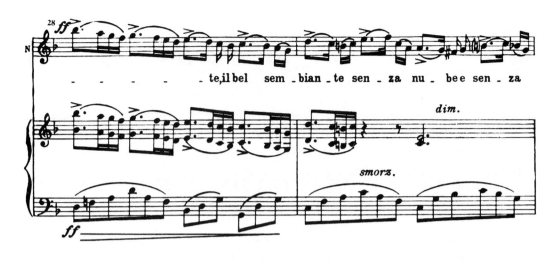

te,il bel sem _ bian _ te sen _ za nu _ be e sen _ za

dim.

smorz.

ff

vel,

OROVESO

Ca _ _ _ sta   Di _ _ _

Soprani

Ca _ sta Di _ va, che i _ nar_gen _ ti que _ ste sa _ creanti _ che

sottovoce

Tenori

Ca _ sta Di _ va, che i _ nar_gen _ ti que _ ste sa _ creanti _ che

Bassi

Ca _ _ _ sta   Di _ _ _

*dolce espressivo e **pp** sempre*

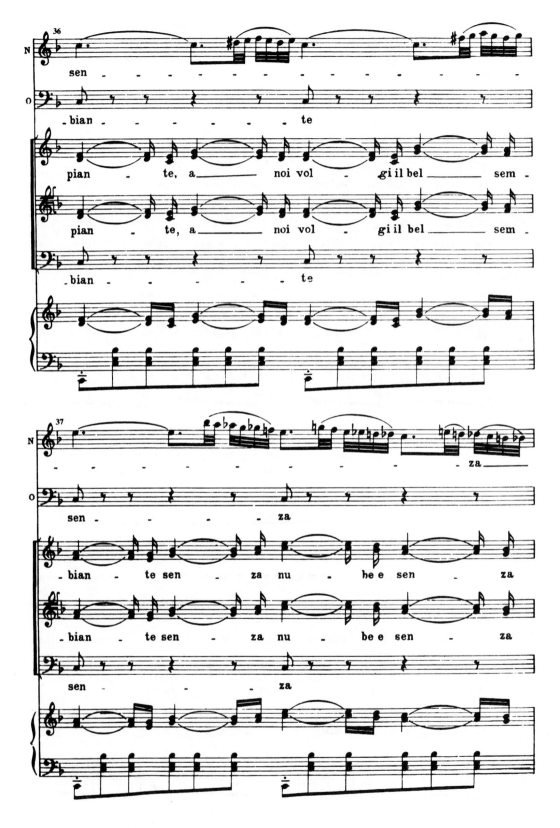

Cabaletta

Allegro (BANDA) *f*

NORMA

All.º assai maestoso

All. assai maestoso

Fi – ne al ri – to; e il sa – cro

(ORCHESTRA) *p e marcate*

bo – sco sia di – sgom – bro – dai – pro – fa – ni.

Quan – do il Nu – me, quando il Nu – me i – ra – to e –

[Recording continues top of page 447.]

NORMA

Casta Diva, che inargenti	Chaste Goddess, who plates with silver
Queste sacre antiche piante,	these sacred ancient plants,
A noi volgi il bel sembiante;	turn your lovely face towards us,
Senza nube e senza vel!	unclouded and unveiled.
Tempra, o Diva, tu de' cori ardenti,	Temper, O Goddess, these ardent hearts,
Tempra ancora lo zelo audace,	o temper their bold zeal.
Spargi in terra, ah, quella pace,	Spread over the earth that peace
Che regnar tu fai nel ciel.	that you make reign in heaven.
Fine al rito; e il sacro bosco	Let the rites be finished and the sacred wood
Sia disgombro dai profani.	be cleared of intruders.
Quando il Nume irato e fosco,	When the angry and gloomy god
Chiegga il sangue dei Romani,	demands the blood of the Romans,
Dal Druidico delubro	from the Druidic shrine
La mia voce tuonerà.	my voice will resound.

TUTTI

Tuoni; e un sol del popol empio	Let it be heard, and let not a single one of the impious race
Non isfugga al giusto scempio;	escape our just massacre,
E primier da noi percosso	and the first to feel our blows,
Il Proconsole cadrà,	the Proconsul will fall.

NORMA

Cadrà . . . punirlo io posso . . .	He will fall . . . punish him I can . . .
(Ma punirlo il cor non sa.)	(But to punish him my heart does not know how.)
(Ah! bello a me ritorna	(Ah, return to me, love,
Del fido amor primiero:	my faithful first love,
E contro il mondo intiero	and, against the entire world
Difesa a te sarò.	I shall be your defense.
Ah! bello a me ritorna	Ah, return to me, love,
Del raggio tuo sereno;	the serene radiance of your gaze;
E vita nel tuo seno	and living in your bosom
E patria e cielo avrò).	both homeland and heaven I'll possess).

CHORUS

Sei lento, si, sei lento,	How it drags on, sluggishly,
O giorno di vendetta;	this day of revenge;
Ma irato il Dio t'affretta	but the angry God hurries you
Che il Tebro condannò.	whom the Tiber condemned.

NORMA

(Ah! bello) . . .	(Ah, return) . . .

CHORUS

Sei lento . . .	How it drags . . .

NORMA

(Ah! riedi ancora	(Ah, return again
Qual eri allora	to what you were then
Quando, ah, quando il cor	when, oh, when my heart
Ti diedi allora).	I gave to you).

—Libretto by FELICE ROMANI

On a libretto by Felice Romani, *Norma* was first performed at the Teatro alla Scala in Milan on December 26, 1831.

Norma, high priestess of the Druids, implores their chaste goddess to bring peace with the Romans. The melody, for fourteen measures of slow $\frac{12}{8}$, seems continually to be seeking a resting point but instead of finding one moves to higher levels of suspense and excitement. The profusion of grace notes, turns, and other embellishments and the broken-chord accompaniment are similar to what we find in some piano music (of Field and Chopin, for example), a medium that was exchanging influences with opera at this time.

The choir echoes Norma's prayer as she sings high coloratura above it. As was becoming conventional, the lyrical cavatina is followed by a cabaletta, an energetic, rhythmically precise aria sung by the same character. Skirting the formalism of this anticipated succession, Bellini interrupts the orchestral introduction with an accompanied recitative. It is this recitative that brings out the struggle in Norma's conscience, for as the chorus cries "Down with the proconsul!" she knows that she cannot comply: the Roman proconsul Pollione is secretly the father of her two children. Although he has deserted her for one of her priestesses, Adalgisa, Norma longs to have him back. As the crowd continues to defame the Romans, Norma prays that Pollione may yet return to her. The aggressive, martial music surrounding her private lyricism epitomizes the crisis she is about to face and at the same time serves to bring the scene to a brilliant close.

GIUSEPPE VERDI (1813–1901)

Il trovatore

Act IV, Scene 1, No. 12: Scene, Aria, and *Miserere*

From *Il trovatore,* ed. Mario Parenti (Milan: Ricordi, 1944), pp. 184–201. Reprinted by permission.

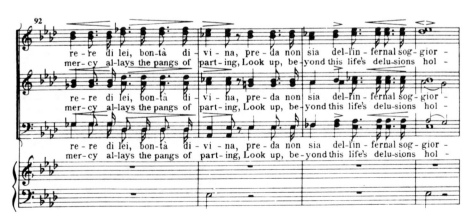

te! _____
thine, _____

di — — o!
mine! _____

re — — re!
soul! _____

re — — re!
soul! _____

re — — re!
soul! _____

(A wing in the palace of Aliaferia. At one end a window barred with iron. A very dark night. Two persons advance, wrapped in cloaks. They are Ruiz and Leonora).

RUIZ
(softly)

Siam giunti:	We have arrived:
Ecco la torre, ove di Stato	here is the tower, where the State's
Gemono i prigionieri! . . . Ah! l'infelice	prisoners moan . . . Ah, unhappy fate,
Ivi fu tratto!	it was here he was brought!

LEONORA

Vanne.	Go.
Lasciami, nè timor di me ti prenda.	Leave me alone, and don't worry about me.
Salvarlo io potrò forse.	Perhaps I'll be able to save him.

(Ruiz goes off)

Timor di me? . . . Sicura,	Fear for me? . . . Surely,
Presta è la mia difesa!	quick is my defense.

(Her eyes fasten on a jewel that ornaments her right hand)

In quest'oscura notte ravvolta,	Enveloped in this dark night,
Presso a te son io, e tu nol sai!	I am near to you, but you do not know it.
Gemente aura, che intorno spiri,	Moaning breeze that spirals around us,
Deh, pietosa gli arreca i miei sospiri!	o, for pity's sake, yield to my sighs!
D'amor sull'ali rosee	On the rose-colored wings of love,
Vanne, sospir dolente,	go, sad sigh,
Del prigioniero misero	the wretched prisoner's
Conforta l'egra mente . . .	sick soul to comfort . . .

Com'aura di speranza	Like a breeze of hope
Aleggia in quella stanza:	flap to that dungeon,
La desta alle memorie,	there to stir those memories,
Ai sogni dell'amor!	arouse dreams of love.
Ma, deh! non dirgli, improvvido,	But, please, tell him not, thoughtlessly,
Le pene del mio cor!	of the troubles of my heart.

LEONORA, MANRICO, & CHORUS

Miserere, d'un alma già vicina	Have mercy for a soul already near
Alla partenza che non ha ritorno.	to the departure that has no return.
Miserere di lei, bontà divina,	Have mercy on him, Divine Goodness,
Preda non sia dell'infernal soggiorno.	that his soul not be victim of infernal sojourn.

LEONORA

Quel suon, quelle preci, solenni, funeste,	That sound, those prayers, solemn, dismal,
Empiron quell'aere di cupo terror!	that tune—they are replete with somber horror.
Contende l'ambascia, che tutta m'investe,	Relieve the agony that overwhelms me,
Al labbro il respiro, i palpiti al cor!	that robs my lips of breath, that makes my heart
	palpitate.

MANRICO

Ah che la morte ognora	Ah, how death is ever
È tarda nel venir,	slow to arrive
A chi desia morir!	to him who desires to die!
Addio, Leonora, addio!	Farewell, Leonora, farewell!

LEONORA

Oh ciel! Sento mancarmi!	O heavens! I feel faint.

CHORUS

Miserere, etc.	Have mercy, etc.

LEONORA

Sull'orrida torre, ahi! par che	Over that horrible tower, alas, it appears that
la morte	death
Con ali di tenebre librando si va!	with its dark wings hovers.
Ah! forse dischiuse gli fian queste porte	Ah, perhaps the doors swing open to death
Sol quando cadaver già freddo sarà!	only when a cadaver is already cold.

MANRICO

Sconto col sangue mio	I expiate with my blood
L'amor che posi in te!	the love that I vowed to you.
Non ti scordar di me!	Forget me not.
Leonora, addio!	Leonora, farewell.

LEONORA

Di te, di te scordarmi!	How could I forget you!

—Libretto by SALVATORE CAMMARANO

Il trovatore, on a libretto by Salvatore Cammarano, based on the play *El trovador* by A. Garcia Gutiérrez, was first performed in Rome on January 19, 1853.

Leonora, led by Manrico's friend Ruiz, has reached the tower of the Aliaferia Palace, where Manrico, her beloved troubadour, is awaiting execution. Two clarinets and two bassoons paint a gloomy scene as the pair approaches. Then Leonora sings unaccompanied of her hope to save Manrico. She continues over string accompaniment, then begins an aria, *D'amor sull'ali rosee* (On the rose-colored wings of love), seeking to console him, yet hiding from him her inner turmoil. She is accompanied by a reduced orchestra, the winds doubling her line in climactic moments. The death knell sounds, and off-stage monks intone an a cappella *Miserere,* praying for the prisoner's soul. The entire orchestra begins a lugubrious march *pianissimo,* to which Leonora sings a lyrical line, interrupted by sobs. When the orchestra stops, we hear Manrico singing to the lute (actually two harps in the orchestra pit), "Ah, che la morte ognora è tarda nel venir" (Ah, how death is ever slow to arrive). His song is interrupted by the funeral music, the chanting of the monks, and Leonora's expressions of terror.

One is reminded of Meyerbeer's handling of similar forces. The gradation and progression from near-speech to higher levels of lyricism display the versatility of Verdi's talent and at the same time his dramatic instinct to avoid the discrete "numbers," formal transitions, and ritornellos that one still finds in Bellini and Rossini.

Carl Maria von Weber (1786–1826)

Der Freischütz

Act II, Finale: Wolf's Glen Scene

Reprinted from *Der Freischütz* (New York: Broude Bros., n.d.).

Samiel Es sei! Bei den Pforten der Hölle! Morgen er oder du! (Verschwindet unter dumpfem Donner)

(K a s p a r richtet sich langsam und erschöpft auf und trocknet sich den Schweiß von der Stirn. Der Hirschfänger mit dem Toten-
kopf ist verschwunden, an dessen Stelle kommt ein kleiner Herd mit glimmenden Kohlen, dabei einige Reißbunde aus der Erde)

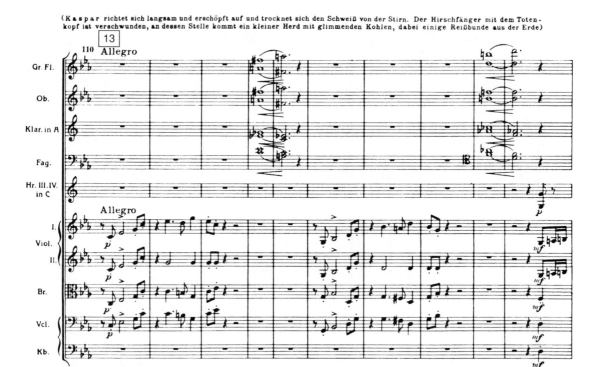

(Max wird auf einer Felsenspitze, dem Wasserfall gegenüber, sichtbar und beugt sich in die Schlucht herab)

Rezitativ

Ha!_____ Fürcht-bar gähnt der düst-re Abgrund! Welch ein Graun, das Au-ge wähnt In ei-nen Höl-lenpfuhl zu

Kaspar (zu Max) Kommst du endlich, Kamerad? Ist das auch | er wird? (Hat das Feuer mit dem Adlerflügel angefacht und erhebt
recht, mich so allein zu lassen? Siehst du nicht, wie mir's sau- | diesen im Gespräch gegen Max)

NB. Diese beiden Wiederholungszeichen sind mit Bleistift im Autograph angegeben und werden nur ausgeführt, wenn Max nicht genug Zeit haben sollte.

Kaspar (wirft ihm die Jagdflasche zu, die Max weglegt) Zuerst trink einmal! Die Nachtluft ist kühl und feucht. Willst du selbst gießen?

Max. Nein, das ist wider die Abrede.

Kaspar. Nicht? So bleib außer dem Kreise, sonst kostet's dein Leben!

Max. Was hab ich zu tun, Hexenmeister?

Kaspar. Fasse Mut! Was du auch hören und sehen magst, verhalte dich ruhig. (Mit eigenem heimlichen Grauen.) Käme vielleicht ein Unbekannter, uns zu helfen, was kümmert es dich? Kommt was anders, was tut's? So etwas sieht ein Gescheiter gar nicht!

Max. O, wie wird das enden!

Kaspar. Umsonst ist der Tod! Nicht ohne Widerstand schenken verborgene Naturen den Sterblichen ihre Schätze. Nur wenn du mich selbst zittern siehst, dann komme mir zu Hilfe und rufe, was ich rufen werde, sonst sind wir beide verloren. (Max macht eine Bewegung des Einwurfs) Still! Die Augenblicke sind kostbar.'(Der Mond ist bis auf einen schmalen Streif verfinstert. Kaspar nimmt die Gießkelle.) Merk auf, was ich hineinwerfen werde, damit du die Kunst lernst! (Er nimmt die Ingredienzen aus der Jagdtasche und wirft sie nach und nach hinein.)

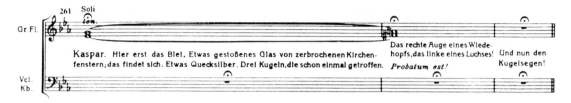

Kaspar. Hier erst das Blei. Etwas gestoßenes Glas von zerbrochenen Kirchenfenstern; das findet sich. Etwas Quecksilber. Drei Kugeln, die schon einmal getroffen. *Probatum est!*

Das rechte Auge eines Wiedehopfs, das linke eines Luchses!

Und nun den Kugelsegen!

MELODRAM

(In drei Pausen sich gegen die Erde neigend) Schütze, der im Dunkeln wacht, Samiel! Samiel! hab acht! Steh mir bei in dieser Nacht, bis der Zauber ist voll-

bracht! Salbe mir so Kraut als Blei, segn es sieben, neun und drei, daß die Kugel tüchtig sei! Samiel! Samiel! herbei!

16

276 Allegro moderato

(Die Masse in der Gießkelle fängt an zu gähren und zu zischen und gibt einen grünlichweißen Schein. Eine Wolke läuft über den Mondstreif, daß die ganze Gegend nur noch von dem Herdfeuer, den Augen der Eule und dem faulen Holz des Baumes erleuchtet ist)

Kaspar (gießt, läßt die Kugel aus der Form fallen und ruft) Eins! Das Echo (wiederholt) Eins!

(Waldvögel kommen herunter, setzen sich um das Feuer, hüpfen und flattern.)

Kaspar (gießt und zählt) Zwei! Echo Zwei!

17

(Ein schwarzer Eber raschelt durchs Gebüsch und jagt wild vorüber.)

(Der ganze Himmel wird schwarze Nacht; die Gewitter treffen furchtbar zusammen. Flammen schlagen aus der Erde. Irrlichter

(Vorhang fällt)

zu Boden)

(Es schlägt eins. Plötzliche Stille. S a m i e l ist verschwunden. K a s p a r liegt noch mit dem Gesicht zu Boden. M a x richtet sich konvulsivisch auf.)

Ende des zweiten Aufzuges

(A frightful glen with a waterfall. A pallid full moon. A storm is brewing. In the foreground a withered tree shattered by lightning seems to glow. In other trees, owls, ravens, and other wild birds. Caspar, without a hat or coat, but with hunting pouch and knife, is laying out a circle of black fieldstones, in the center of which lies a skull. A few steps away, a hacked-off eagle wing, a ladle, and bullet molds.)

CHORUS OF INVISIBLE SPIRITS

Milch des Mondes fiel auf's Kraut	The milk of the moon fell on the herbs.
Uhui! Uhui!	Uhui! Uhui!
Spinnweb' ist mit Blut bethaut!	Spider webs dabbed with blood.
Eh' noch wieder Abend graut,	Before another evening darkens,
Ist sie todt, die zarte Braut!	will she die, the lovely bride.
Eh' noch wieder sinkt die Nacht,	Before another night falls,
Ist das Opfer dargebracht!	will the sacrifice be offered.
Uhui! Uhui! Uhui!	Uhui! Uhui! Uhui!

(A clock in the distance strikes twelve. The circle of stones is completed.)

CASPAR

Samiel! Samiel! erschein!	Samiel, Samiel, appear!
Bei des Zaub'rers Hirngebein!	By the wizard's skull-bone,
Samiel! Samiel! erschein!	Samiel, Samiel, appear!

SAMIEL *(steps out of a rock)*

Was rufst du?	Why do you call?

CASPAR *(throws himself at Samiel's feet)*

Du weisst, dass meine Frist	You know that my days of grace
Schier abgelaufen ist.	are coming to an end.

SAMIEL

Morgen!	Tomorrow!

CASPAR

Verläng're sie noch einmal mir!	Will you extend them once more?

SAMIEL

Nein!	No!

CASPAR

Ich bringe neue Opfer dir.	I bring you new sacrifices.

SAMIEL

Welche?	Which ones?

CASPAR

Mein Jagdgesell, er naht,	My hunting companion—he approaches—
Er, der noch nie dein dunkles Reich betrat.	he who has never before set foot in your dark kingdom.

SAMIEL

Was sein Begehr?   What does he want?

CASPAR

Freikugeln sind's, auf die er Hoffnung baut.   Magic bullets, in which he puts his hope.

SAMIEL

Sechse treffen, sieben äffen!   Six strike, seven deceive!

CASPAR

Die siebente sei dein: The seventh is yours:
Aus seinem Rohr lenk' sie nach seiner Braut!   From his own gun it will aim at his bride.
Dies wird ihn der Verzweiflung weih'n,   That will drive him to despair,
Ihn und den Vater.   both he and his father.

SAMIEL

Noch hab' ich keinen Teil an ihr.   I side with neither party.

CASPAR *(afraid)*

Genügt er dir allein?   Will he be sufficient for you?

SAMIEL

Das findet sich!   Perhaps.

CASPAR

Doch schenkst du Frist,   If you will grant me grace
Und wieder auf drei Jahr,   for another three years,
Bring' ich ihn dir zu Beute dar?!   Will I bring him to you as prey?!

SAMIEL

Es sei! Bei den Pforten der Hölle!   So be it. By the gates of hell,
Morgen Er oder Du!   Tomorrow: he or you!

(He disappears amidst thunder. Also the skull and knife disappear. In their place a small stove with glowing coals is seen.)

CASPAR

Trefflich bedient!   Splendidly served.
(He takes a drink from his canteen.)

Gesegn' es Samiel!   Thank you, Samiel.
Er hat mir warm gemacht!   It warms my heart.
Aber wo bleibt denn Max?   But what is keeping Max?
Sollte er wortbrüchig werden?   Would he break his word?
Samiel hilf?   Help, Samiel!

(He puts more wood on the coals and blows at it. Owls and other birds flap their wings, as if they wanted to fan the fire. The fire smokes and crackles.)

MAX (*appears on top of a rock, opposite the waterfall; he looks down into the glen*)

Ha! Furchtbar gähnt	Ah, how frightful yawns
Der düst're Abgrund! Welch' ein Grau'n!	this gloomy abyss! How dreadful!
Das Auge wähnt	The eyes fancy
In einen Höllenpfuhl zu schau'n!	seeing a pool of hell.
Wie dort sie Wetterwolken ballen,	Behold the storm clouds forming.
Der Mond verliert von seinem Schein,	The moonlight is dimming.
Gespenst'ge Nebelbilder wallen,	Ghostly, misty apparitions float in.
Belebt ist das Gestein,	The stones appear alive,
Und hier Husch! husch!	And here hush, hush,
Fliegt Nachtgevögel Auf in Busch!	the nightbirds fly into the bush.
Rotgraue, narb'ge Zweige Strecken	Scarred red-gray boughs stretch
Nach mir die Riesenfaust!	their giant claws at me.
Nein! Ob da Herz auch graust	No. Whether the heart feels horror or not
Ich muss! ich trotze allen Schrecken.	I must! despite all the terrors.

CASPAR (*aside*)

Dank, Samiel! die Frist is gewonnen.	Thanks, Samiel, the grace period is granted.

(*to Max*)

Kommst du endlich, Kamerad? Ist das	You have finally arrived, friend?
euch recht, mich so allein zu lassen	Was it right to make me wait so long?
Siehst du nicht, wie mir's sauer wird?	Can't you see how painful it has been?

(*He fans the fire with the eagle's wing.*)

MAX (*staring at the wing*)

Ich schoss den Adler aus hoher Luft.	I shot the eagle at a higher altitude.
Ich kann nicht rückwärts, mein Schicksal ruft!	I cannot ask my fate to march in reverse.

(*He climbs a few steps, then stands still, gazing fixedly at the opposite rock.*)

Weh mir!	Help me!

CASPAR

So komm doch, die Zeit eilt!	Come on, time flies!

MAX

Ich kann nicht hinab!	I can't go ahead.

CASPAR

Hasenherz! Klimmst ja sonst wie eine Gemse!	Coward! You always climbed like a mountain goat.

MAX

Sie dort hin, sieh!	See there, see!

(*He points to the moonlit rock. A white and worn-out female form becomes evident, raising her hands.*)

Was dort sich weist, ist meiner Mutter Geist.	What you see there is my mother's ghost.
So lag sie im Sarg, so ruht sie im Grab.	She lies in the coffin, resting in the grave.
Sie fleht mit warnendem Blick,	She implores with a cautioning glimpse.
Sie winkt mir zurück!	She nods to me to return.

CASPAR (*to himself*)

Hilf, Samiel!	Help, Samiel!

(aloud)

Alberne Fratzen! Ha! Ha! Ha!	Silly fools! Ha! ha! ha!
Sieh noch einmal hin, damit du die	Look once more, and recognize
Folgen deiner feigen Torheit erkennst!	your faint-hearted folly.

(The vision disappears. Agathe's form now is apparent, her hair disheveled and adorned with leaves and straw. She acts like a madwoman about to throw herself into the abyss.)

MAX

Agathe! Sie springt in dens Fluss!	Agathe. She is jumping into the river.
Hinab! Hinab!	Go to her. Go to her.
Ich muss! Agathe! Hinab ich muss!	I must! Agathe, I must go down.
Hinab! Ich muss!	I must!

(The moon darkens. The apparition evaporates. Max climbs down.)

CASPAR *(jeering, to himself)*

Ich denke wohl auch, du musst!	I think likewise, you must.

MAX *(forcefully to Caspar)*

Hier bin ich! Was hab ich zu tun?	Here I am. What do I have to do?

CASPAR *(hands him the canteen, which Max puts aside)*

Zuerst trink' einmal! Die Nachtluft ist	First drink. The night air is cold
kühl und feucht. Willst du selbst giessen?	and damp. Do you want to cast the bullets yourself?

MAX

Nein! das ist wider die Abrede!	No, that was not the agreement.

CASPAR

Nicht? So bleib' ausser dem Kreise,	No? Then stay outside of the circle,
sonst kostet's dein Leben!	or it will cost you your life!

MAX

Was hab' ich zu tun, Hexenmeister?	What must I do, Wizard?

CASPAR

Fasse Mut! Was du auch hören und sehen magst,	Courage! Whatever you hear or see, stay calm.
vehalte dich ruhig. Käme vielleicht ein	Should a stranger come to help us, don't let it bother
Unbekannter, uns zu helfen, was kümmert's dich?	you. Whatever happens, fear not. If you are wise, you
Kommt was andres, was tut's? So etwas sieht ein	will pay no attention.
Gescheidter nicht.	

MAX

O, wie wird das enden!	How will this ever end?

CASPAR

Umsonst ist der Tod! Nicht ohne Widerstand	Death is in vain. Not without resistance will the
schenken verborgene Naturen den Sterblichen ihre	invisible powers give up their treasures. But when

Schätze. Nur du mich selbst zittern siehst, dann komm' mir zu Hülfe und rufe, was ich rufen werde, sonst sind wir beide verloren.

you see me falter, then come to my aid and repeat the call that I make; otherwise we shall both be lost.

(Max stirs to raise an objection.)

Still! Die Augenblicke sind kostbar!

Be quiet. The moments are precious.

(The moon is barely visible. Caspar seizes the crucible.)

Merk' auf, was ich hineinwerfen werde, damit du die Kunst lernst.

Now mark me, that you may learn the art.

(He takes the ingredients from his pouch and throws them in one by one.)

Hier erst das Blei. Etwas Glas von zerbrochnen Kirchenfenstern, das findet sich. Etwas Quecksilber. Drei Kugeln, die schon einmal getroffen. Das rechte Auge eines Wiedehopfs, das linke eines Luchses— *Probatum est!* Und nun den Kugelsegen!

First, then, the lead. Then this piece of glass from a broken church window, some mercury, three balls that have already hit the mark. The right eye of a lapwing, and the left of a lynx. *Probatum est!* Now to bless the balls.

MELODRAMA

CASPAR *(pausing three times, bowing to the earth)*

Schütze, der im Dunken wacht,
Samiel! Samiel! Hab' acht!
Steh mir bei in dieser Nacht,
Bis der Zauber ist vollbracht!
Salbe mir so Kraut als Blei,
Segn' es sieben, neun und drei,
Dass die Kugel tüchtig sei!
Samiel! Samiel! Herbei!

Hunter, who watches in the darkness,
Samiel! Samiel! Pay attention!
Stay with me through this night
until the magic is achieved.
Anoint for me the herbs and lead.
Bless the seven, nine and three,
so that the bullet will be fit.
Samiel! Samiel! Come to me!

(The material in the crucible begins to hiss and bubble, sending forth a greenish flame. A cloud passes over the moon, obscuring the light.)

(casts the first bullet, which drops in the pan)

Eins!

One!

(The echo repeats: Eins! *Nightbirds crowd around the fire.)*

Zwei!

Two!

(The echo repeats: Zwei! *A black boar passes)*
(startled, he counts)

Drei!

Three!

(Echo: Drei! *A storm starts to rage)*
(continues to count anxiously)

Vier!

Four!

(Echo: Vier! *Cracking of whips and the sound of galloping horses is heard)*
(more and more alarmed)

Funf!

Five!

(Echo: Fünf! *Dogs barking and horses neighing are heard: the devil's hunt.)*

Wehe! Das wilde Heer!	Woe is me! The wild chase!

CHORUS

Durch Berg und Tal,	Through hill and dale,
Durch Schlund und Schacht,	through glen and mire,
Durch Tau und Wolken,	through dew and cloud,
Sturm und Nacht!	storm and night!
Durch Höhle, Sumpf und Erdenkluft,	Through marsh, swamp, and chasm,
Durch Feuer, Erde, See und Luft,	through fire, earth, sea, and air,
Jo ho! Wau wau! Jo ho! Wau wau!	Yo ho! Bow wow! Yo ho! Bow wow!
Jo ho ho ho ho ho ho ho!	Yo ho ho ho ho ho ho ho!

—Libretto by FRIEDRICH KIND

CASPAR

Sechs!	Six!

(Echo: Sechs! *Deepest darkness. The storm lashes with terrific force.)*

Samiel! Samiel! Samiel! Hilf!	Samiel! Samiel! Samiel! Help!

SAMIEL *(appears)*

Hier bin ich!	Here I am.

(Caspar is hurled to the ground)

MAX

(nearly losing his balance from the impact of the storm; he jumps out of the magic circle and grips a dead branch, shouting)

Samiel!	Samiel!

(The storm suddenly dies down. Instead of the dead tree, the black hunter appears before Max, grabbing his hand.)

SAMIEL

Hier bin ich!	Here I am.

(Max makes the sign of the cross as he is thrown to the ground. The clock strikes one. Dead silence. Samiel has disappeared. Caspar remains motionless, face to the ground. Max rises convulsively.)

Supernatural incidents, a natural setting, and human actions intertwine in this pioneering work of German Romantic opera, first performed in Berlin in 1821. Johann Friedrich Kind based the libretto on a story by Johann August Apel, who in turn depended on <u>folklore</u> and the <u>model of Goethe's *Faust*.</u>

Caspar, Max's unsuccessful rival for the love of Agathe, has sold his soul to the devil, who has taken the form of Samiel, the legendary Black Huntsman. To get Max's soul for the devil, Caspar persuades Max to make a deal: Max can earn the right to marry Agathe if he will use a magic bullet to win a marksmanship contest. The magic bullets Caspar supplies will obey the user's wish, but one is controlled by Samiel, who has destined it to kill Agathe. Caspar keeps three of the seven bullets cast, giving four to Max, who uses up three bullets before the contest begins, so Max has only one left (that guided by Samiel) for the fateful trial. Although Agathe unexpectedly appears in the line of fire as Max shoots, she is protected by an old hermit's magical wreath. The bullet kills Caspar instead, and all ends well.

The magic bullets are cast in the eerie midnight Wolf's Glen scene. The somber forest background is depicted diabolically through suggestive orchestration and a harmonic scheme that contrasts F♯ minor and C minor. Caspar's song-speech, "Du weisst, dass meine Frist schier abgelaufen ist" (You know that my days of grace are coming to an end, measure 51), is almost Wagnerian in its single-minded orchestral development of a motive against the voice, which seems to draw its tones from the orchestra rather than being accompanied by it. Samiel frequently interrupts (in normal speaking voice) to lay down the terms for the granting of the magic bullets.

Particularly notable in this scene is the *melodrama* of the casting of the bullets (measures 264–430). *Melodrama* was a genre of musical theater that combined spoken dialogue with music in the background. Here Caspar's lines are spoken over continuous orchestral music. First he evokes Samiel; then as he casts each bullet, with Max cowering beside him, Caspar counts *eins, zwei, drei,* etc., and the mountains echo each count. For each casting Weber painted a different miniature nature-picture of the terrifying setting and wildlife of the dark forest: for the first bullet the greenish light of the moon partly hidden by a cloud; for the second a wild bird hovering above the fire; for the third a black boar running wild and startling Caspar; for the fourth a storm brewing and breaking out; for the fifth galloping horses and whips cracking; for the sixth barking dogs and neighing horses. At this point an unseen unison chorus of wild hunters sings in a monotone and Caspar shouts "Six!" Before the casting of the fatal seventh bullet, the music of Max's aria from Act I breaks in, above which Caspar shouts "Seven!" (measure 408). Throughout, Weber ingeniously deployed the resources of his orchestra: timpani, trombones, clarinets, and horns in the foreground, often against string tremolos. Shocking diminished and augmented intervals and daring chromaticism are prominent in the melody and harmony.

RICHARD WAGNER (1813–1883)

Tristan und Isolde

Act I, Scene 5 (excerpt)

From *Tristan und Isolde,* ed. Felix Mottl (Frankfurt: Peters, 1914), pp. 85–102. Reprinted by permission.

und heften ihn wieder mit steigender Sehnsucht auf einander.)

Isolde (mit bebender Stimme) — (an seine Brust sinkend)

Tri - stan!   Tristan (überströmend)   Treu - lo - ser Hol - der!

I - sol - de!

108. (Er umfaßt sie mit Glut.)

Tristan   (Sie verbleiben in stummer Umarmung.)

Se - ligste Frau!

Lebhaft mit Steigerung

(Brangäne, die mit abgewandtem Gesicht, voll Verwirrung und Schauder
sich über den Bord gelehnt hatte, wendet sich jetzt dem Anblick des in

Tenor II

Alle Männer (außen)   Heil!   Kö - nig
Baß I   Heil!   Kö - nig

Baß II

Heil!   Kö - nig Mar - ke Heil!

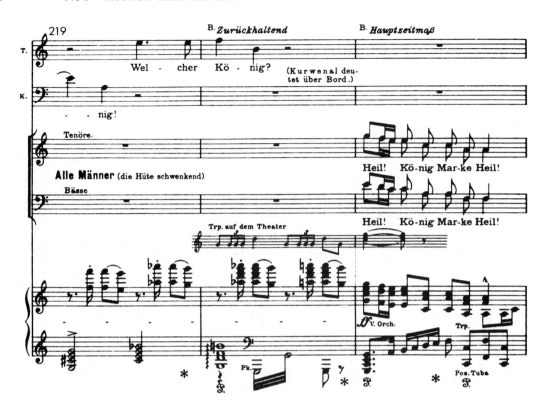

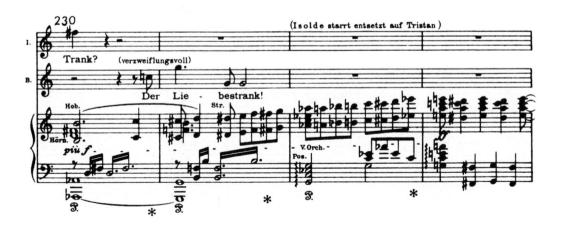

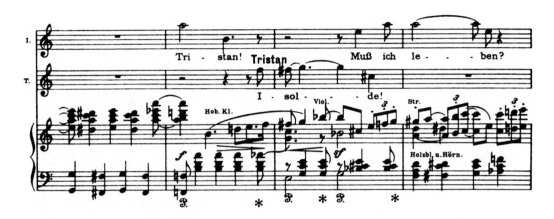

SAILORS *(outside)*

Auf das Tau!	Haul the line.
Anker ab!	Drop the anchor.

TRISTAN *(starting wildly)*

Los den Anker!	Drop the anchor.
Das Steuer dem Strom!	Stern to the current.
Den Winden Segel und Mast!	Sail and mast to the wind.

(He takes the cup from Isolde)

Wohl kenn' ich Irlands	Well know I Ireland's
Königin,	Queen,
Und ihrer Künste	and her art's
Wunderkraft:	magic.
Den Balsam nützt' ich,	The balsam I used
Den sie bot:	that she brought.
Den Becher nehm' ich nun,	The goblet I now take
Dass ganz ich heut' genese.	so that I might altogether today recover.
Und achte auch	And heed also
Des Sünne Eid's,	the oath of atonement,
Den ich zum Dank dir sage.	which I thankfully made to you.
Tristans Ehre,	Tristan's honor,
Höchste Treu!	highest truth.
Tristans Elend,	Tristan's anguish,
Kühnster Trotz!	brave defiance.
Trug des Herzens!	Betrayal of the heart,
Traum der Ahnung:	Dream of presentiment,
Ew'ger Trauer	eternal sorrow,
Einz'ger Trost:	unique solace,
Vergessens güt'ger Trank,	forgetting's kindly draught,
Dich trink' ich sonder Wank.	I drink without wavering.

(He sits and drinks)

ISOLDE

Betrug auch hier?	Betrayed even in this?
Mein die Hälfte!	The half is mine!

(She wrests the cup from his hand)

Verräter! Ich trink' sie dir!	Traitor, I drink to you!

*(She drinks, and then throws away the cup. Both, seized with shuddering, gaze at each other with deepest
agitation, still with stiff demeanor, as the expression of defiance of death fades into a glow of passion.
Trembling grips them. They convulsively clutch their hearts and pass their hands over their brows.
Then they seek each other with their eyes, sink into confusion, and once more turn with renewed longing
toward each other)*

ISOLDE *(with wavering voice)*

Tristan!	Tristan!

TRISTAN *(overwhelmed)*

Isolde!	Isolde!

ISOLDE *(sinking on his chest)*

Treuloser Holder!	Treacherous lover!

TRISTAN

Seligste Frau!   Divine woman!

(He embraces her with ardor. They remain in silent embrace)

ALL THE MEN *(outside)*

Heil! Heil!   Hail! Hail!
König Marke!   King Mark!
König Marke, Heil!   King Mark, hail!

BRANGÄNE

*(who, with averted face, full of confusion and horror, had leaned over the side, turns to see the
pair sunk into a love embrace, and hurls herself, wringing her hands, into the foreground)*

Wehe! Weh!   Woe's me! Woe's me!
Unabwendbar   Inevitable,
Ew'ge Not   endless distress,
Für kurzen Tod!   instead of quick death!
Tör'ger Treue   Misleading truth,
Trugvolles Werk   deceitful work
Blüht nun jammernd empor!   now blossoms pitifully upward.

(They break from their embrace)

TRISTAN *(bewildered)*

Was träumte mir   What did I dream
Von Tristans Ehre?   of Tristan's honor?

ISOLDE

Was träumte mir   What did I dream
Von Isoldes Schmach?   of Isolde's disgrace?

TRISTAN

Du mir verloren?   Are you lost to me?

ISOLDE

Du mich verstossen?   Have you repulsed me?

TRISTAN

Trügenden Zaubers Tückische List?   False magic's nasty trick!

ISOLDE

Törigen Zürnes Eitles Dräu'n!   Foolish wrath's vain menace!

TRISTAN

Isolde! Süsseste Maid!   Isolde, sweetest maiden!

ISOLDE

Tristan! Trautester Mann!   Tristan; most beloved man!

BOTH

Wie sich die Herzen wogend erheben,   How, heaving, our hearts are uplifted!

Wie alle Sinne wonnig erbeben!	How all our senses blissfully quiver!
Sehnender Minne	Longing, passion,
Schwellendes Blühen,	swelling, blooms
Schmachtender Liebe	languishing love,
Seliges Glühen!	blessed glow!
Jach in der Brust	Precipitate in the breast
Jauchzende Lust!	exulting desire!
Isolde! Tristan!	Isolde! Tristan!
Tristan! Isolde!	Tristan! Isolde!
Welten entronnen	Escaped from the world,
Du mir gewonnen!	you have won me.
Du mir einzig bewusst,	You, my only thought,
Höchste Liebeslust!	highest love's desire!

(The curtains are now drawn wide apart. The entire ship is filled with knights and sailors,
who joyfully signal the shore from aboard. Nearby is seen a cliff crowned by a castle.
Tristan and Isolde remain lost in mutual contemplation, unaware of what is taking place)

BRANGÄNE
(to the women, who at her bidding ascend from below)

Schnell den Mantel,	Quick, the cloak,
Den Königsschmuck!	the royal robe.

(rushing between Tristan and Isolde)

Unsel'ge! Auf!	Up, unfortunate pair! Up!
Hört, wo wir sind.	See where we are!

(She puts the royal cloak on Isolde, who does not notice anything)

ALL THE MEN

Heil! Heil!	Hail, hail!
König Marke!	King Mark!
König Marke, Heil!	King Mark, hail!

KURWENAL *(advancing cheerfully)*

Heil Tristan!	Hail, Tristan!
Glücklicher Held!	Fortunate hero!
Mit reichem Hofgesinde	With splendid courtiers
Dort auf Nachen	there in the skiff
Naht Herr Marke.	Mark approaches.
Heil! wie die Fahrt ihn freut,	Ah, how the ride delights him,
Dass er die Braut sich freit!	for soon he will be wooing the bride.

TRISTAN *(looking up, bewildered)*

Wer naht?	Who comes?

KURWENAL

Der König!	The King.

TRISTAN

Welcher König?	Which King?

(Kurwenal points over the side. Tristan stares stupefied at the shore)

ALL THE MEN *(waving their hats)*

Heil! König Marke!	Hail, King Mark!

ISOLDE *(confused)*

Marke! Was will er?	Mark! What does he want?
Was ist, Brangäne!	What is that, Brangäne?
Welcher Ruf?	What is the shouting?

BRANGÄNE

Isolde! Herrin!	Isolde! Mistress,
Fassung nur heut!	get hold of yourself.

ISOLDE

Wos bin ich? Leb' ich?	Where am I? Am I alive?
Ha! Welcher Trank?	Oh, what drink was it?

BRANGÄNE *(despairingly)*

Der Liebestrank!	The love potion.

ISOLDE *(stares, frightened, at Tristan)*

Tristan!	Tristan!

TRISTAN

Isolde!	Isolde!

ISOLDE *(She falls, fainting, upon his chest)*.

Muss ich leben?	Must I live?

BRANGÄNE *(to the women)*

Helft der Herrin!	Help your mistress!

TRISTAN

O Wonne voller Tücke!	O rapture full of cunning!
O Truggeweihtes Glücke!	O fraudulently won good fortune!

ALL THE MEN *(in a general acclamation)*

Heil dem König	Hail the King!
Kornwall, Heil!	Hail, Cornwall!

(People have climbed over the ship's side, others have extended a bridge, and the atmosphere is one of expectation of the arrival of those that have been awaited, as the curtain falls).

Wagner wrote his own libretto, basing it on a thirteenth-century romance by Gottfried von Strassburg. He believed that the libretto should serve mainly as a framework for the music, and that poetry, scenic design, staging, action, and music should work together to form what he called a *Gesamtkunstwerk* (total or joint artwork). He considered the action of the drama to have an inner and an outer aspect, the orchestra conveying the inner, the sung words the outer aspect or action. The music is continuous throughout each act, not formally divided into recitatives, arias, and other set numbers. This music is constructed out of *Leitmotifs,* motives that are associated with persons, events, feelings, and objects in the play. Wagner worked on the poem and the music between 1857 and 1859. *Tristan und Isolde* was first performed in Munich on June 21, 1868.

This scene, in which Tristan and Isolde fall in love, demonstrates the effective interweaving of action, scenery, and musical forces. The shipboard gear, sails, lines, Isolde's private quarters, and the nearby shore objectify Tristan's assigned mission, to deliver the reluctant Isolde to King Mark as his bride. As the ship's crew drops anchor and hails the waiting King on shore, the two lovers, oblivious of the excitement around them, succumb to the love potion substituted by Brangäne for the poison Isolde demanded and which they shared. The chorus, with its realistic shouts, interrupts the declamation, sometimes speechlike, sometimes lyrical and passionate, of Tristan and Isolde. The large orchestra maintains continuity throughout the action but elaborates within each segment of the text motives appropriate to the content of the speeches or underlying emotions and associations. Thus action, dialogue, musical scene painting, and lyrical expression are not parceled out to different moments of music, but all are constantly mingled, reinforcing each other.

Some details concerning the introduction of motives and their development merit attention. At measure 38 the motive of Tristan's honor is introduced and identified by the sung text, "Tristans Ehre, höchste Treu!" (Tristan's honor, highest truth). It will be developed later. As Isolde begins to drink the potion (measure 64), she sings "Ich trink' sie dir!" (I drink to you), to a rising major sixth, followed by a descending semitone, a motive from here on associated with the love potion. (In the opening of the prelude to the first act, this motive has a major sixth rather than a minor sixth.) The orchestra takes up the motive and provides a new twist through ascending semitones that suggest mutual longing. Wagner at this point provided music for a pantomime, prescribing particular gestures and actions by the two characters to perform at specific points in the music.

The climactic moment is reached at measure 102, when the two stare longingly at each other, and the rising chromatic motive is accompanied by a progression from a dominant-ninth chord to a deceptive F-major harmony instead of the expected A minor, symbolizing perhaps the foiled death wish. (This progression returns at measures 172 and 247.) Now Isolde and Tristan call to each other, and a new motive (measure 103) is developed in the violas and cellos. At the words "Sehnender Minne" (passionate love), which they pronounce together (measure 160), a still further motive is thereby identified and churned through a series of rising sequences. The celebratory music hailing the King increasingly competes for attention with the continued rapture of the lovers until the curtain falls at the end of Act I (measures 254–58).

HUGO WOLF (1859–1903)

125

Kennst du das Land

From Wolf, *Ausgewählte Lieder,* ed. Elena Gerhardt (Frankfurt: Peters, 1932), pp. 134–41. Reprinted by permission.

Kennst du das Land, wo die Zitronen blühn,

Im dunklen Laub die Gold-Orangen glühn,
Ein sanfter Wind vom blauen Himmel weht,
Die Myrte still und hoch der Lorbeer steht?
Kennst du es wohl? Dahin, dahin
Möcht' ich mit dir, o mein Geliebter, ziehn.

Kennst du das Haus? Auf Säulen ruht sein Dach,
Es glänzt der Saal, es schimmert das Gemach,
Und Marmorbilder Stehn und sehn mich an:
Was hat man dir, du armes Kind, getan?
Kennst du es wohl? Dahin, dahin
Möcht' ich mit dir, o mein Beschützer, ziehn.

Kennst du den Berg und seinen Wolkensteg?
Das Maultier sucht im Nebel seinen Weg;
In Höhlen wohnt der Drachen alte Brut;
Es stürzt der Fels und über ihn die Flut.
Kennst du ihn wohl? Dahin, dahin
Geht unser Weg! o Vater, lass uns ziehn!

Do you know the land where the lemon trees
    blossom?
Among dark leaves the golden oranges glow.
A gentle breeze from blue skies drifts.
The myrtle is still, and the laurel stands high.
Do you know it well? There, there
would I go with you, my beloved.

Do you know the house? On pillars rests its roof.
The great hall glistens, the room shines,
and the marble statues stand and look at me, asking:
"What have they done to you, poor child?"
Do you know it well? There, there
would I go with you, O my protector.

Do you know the mountain and its path?
The mule searches in the fog for his way;
In the caves dwells the dragon of the old breed.
The cliff falls, and over it the flood.
Do you know it well? There, there
leads our way, O father, let us go!

Mignon's song *Kennst du das Land?* in Goethe's *Wilhelm Meister* was a favorite among composers; both Schubert and Schumann had also set it to music. Mignon is dreaming of her homeland in Italy, from which she had been abducted, and wishes that she could go back with her protector, Wilhelm. Wolf in 1888 used a modified strophic form for its three stanzas. The singer's line, though it is in an arioso, almost recitative style rather than in periodic melodic phrases, always preserves a truly vocal character. Continuity, however, as in Wagner's work, is sustained in the instrumental part rather than the voice. For example, in the last strophe, while the key changes from G♭ major to F♯ minor (measure 78), Wolf, departing from the previous strophes, maintains a thread by continuing to develop the same motive as before in the right hand. The chromatic voice-leading, appoggiaturas, anticipations, and the wandering tonality are clearly inspired by the idiom of *Tristan*.

126 GUSTAV MAHLER (1860–1911)

Kindertotenlieder

No. 1, *Nun will die Sonn' so hell aufgehen*

Reprinted from Edition Eulenburg, 1988.

126 MAHLER *Kindertotenlieder*

- licht _____   der Welt!

Nun will die Sonn' so hell aufgeh'n,	Now will the sun so brightly rise again,
Als sei kein Unglück die Nacht gescheh'n!	as if no misfortune occurred during the night.
Das Unglück geschah nur mir allein!	The misfortune happened to me alone.
Die Sonne, sie scheinet allgemein!	The sun shines for everyone.
Du musst nicht die Nacht in dir verschränken,	You must not become tangled up with the night in yourself,
Musst sie ins ew'ge Licht versenken!	You must be immersed in perennial light.
Ein Lämplein verlosch in meinem Zelt!	A little lamp went out in my tent.
Heil sei dem Freudenlicht der Welt.	Blessed be the joyous light of the world.

—FRIEDRICH RÜCKERT

The *Kindertotenlieder* of 1901–04 is a cycle of five songs for solo voice and orchestra on poems of Friedrich Rückert that deal with the death of children and with the feelings of grieving parents. (Rückert wrote the poems after his own two children died from scarlet fever.) *Nun will die Sonn' so hell aufgehen* (Now the sun will rise again) is through-composed, but the last two lines of the second stanza rework the music of the parallel lines of the first. They convey the comforting message that despite the tragic death, the cheering light of the sun continues to bless the world.

Mahler achieved a transparent, chamberlike sound; the sparse use of instruments allows the delicate counterpoint to shine through. This counterpoint assumes the underlying harmonic flow of post-Wagnerian chromatic harmony, which, stripped here to its bare essentials, gains a freshness and clarity that is uncharacteristic of this often turgid compositional idiom.

127 RICHARD STRAUSS (1864–1949)

Don Quixote, Op. 35

Themes, and Variations I and II

a) Don Quixote's theme

b) Sancho Panza's theme

c) Variation 1

d) Variation 2

This symphonic poem, composed in 1896 and 1897, is an instrumental dramatization of Miguel de Cervantes's picaresque novel of 1605 about a bungling hero, Don Quixote, who imagines himself a knight; his horse, Rosinante; and his servant, Sancho Panza. In one adventure, Don Quixote imagines fighting giants, but they are actually windmills, and in another a flock of sheep in the dusty plain appears to him to be an army he must battle to defend a weaker brigade.

After a prologue that is virtually a miniature symphonic poem, the two principal themes are set forth in two separate sections: *Don Quixote, der Ritter von der traurigen Gestalt* (Don Quixote, the knight of the sorrowful countenance), in which the knight's theme, in D minor, is stated mainly in a solo cello; and *Sancho Panza,* whose theme, in F major, is in the bass clarinet, often joined by the bass tuba. Some motives in the solo viola and oboe suggest Rosinante. Ten "fantastic" variations and an Epilogue make up the remainder of the piece.

Much of this work was conceived in contrapuntal lines, and the association of the themes with particular solo instruments gives the texture a transparent clarity. These variations do not preserve a melody or harmonic progression and its form through a number of statements; rather, the themes of the two main characters are subjected to transformations in which the head of the theme usually leads to the unfolding of a new melodic character.

The first variation is built on a scaffolding supplied by transformations of the two main themes in their characteristic instruments. We overhear an abstract and sometimes abstruse conversation, which leads to the tilting with windmills. The second variation of the knight's theme portrays in the rather impotent strings Don Quixote's attempts to be bold and heroic, but they are immediately ridiculed by the winds' mocking transformation of the Sancho theme. The encounter with the sheep takes up most of this variation, and here Strauss anticipates the technique Schoenberg called *Klangfarbenmelodie,* in which instruments maintaining constant pitches drop in and out of an orchestral texture, creating a melody of tone colors (measures 93–125). (Schoenberg experimented with this method in *Farben,* which he later called *Summer Morning by a Lake,* the third of *Five Orchestral Pieces,* Op. 16, of 1909.) Strauss's changing colors transport us into a dream world, where the normal dimensions of melody and harmony no longer pertain. "Fantastic" is an apt word for these variations, where familiar themes and relationships lose their normal thread and footing.

Modest Musorgsky (1839–1881)

Bez solntsa (Sunless)

No. 3, *Okonchen prazdnyi, shumnyi den'* (The idle, noisy day is over)

вер - кый друг ми - нув - ших дней, Скло - ни - лась ти - хо к из - го - ло - вью. И

сме - ло от - дал ей сд - ной Всю ду - шу я вс ле -

зе без - молвной, Ни - кем не зри - мой, сча - стья

пол_ ной,   В сле_ зе,   дав но хра ни   мной! —

The idle, noisy day is over;
grown silent, humankind slumbers.
All is quiet. The shadow of the May night
engulfs the sleeping capital.
But sleep escapes me,
and by the rays of another dawn
my mind leafs
through the pages of lost years.
As if renewed, breathing the poison
of springtime's passionate dreams,
I resurrect in my soul a series of
hopes, desires, delusions . . . .

Alas, they are but phantoms!
I am bored with their lifeless crush,
and the noise of their old chatter
no longer has any power over me.
Only one shadow of all the shadows
appeared to me breathing with love,
as a faithful friend of days gone by
bent gently towards my pillow.
Boldly I surrendered to her alone
all my soul in silent tears
seen by no one, full of happiness . . .
in tears that I have long conserved.

This song is remarkable for its harmonic successions, such as the G♭-major triad going directly to a seventh chord on G (measures 6–7, 14). Such juxtapositions and also certain simultaneous combinations appear to be chosen for their color rather than for their direction. The tonality remains clearly C major, which is reaffirmed repeatedly (measures 8, 10, 15–23, 30, 37, and in the final cadence). Yet the narrow-gauged melody, which stays within a fifth against rapidly shifting chords, perversely introduces B♭ and A♭ in defiance of the tonality of C. And between the C anchors Musorgsky's harmony roams all over the chromatic scale and in one place in the vocal line (measures 35–36) suggests the whole-tone scale. (See also the commentary on Debussy's *Nuages,* NAWM 131, where it is shown that the accompaniment figure of measures 16ff. is borrowed.)

129 ALEXANDER SKRYABIN (1872–1915)

Vers la flamme, Poème pour piano, Op. 72

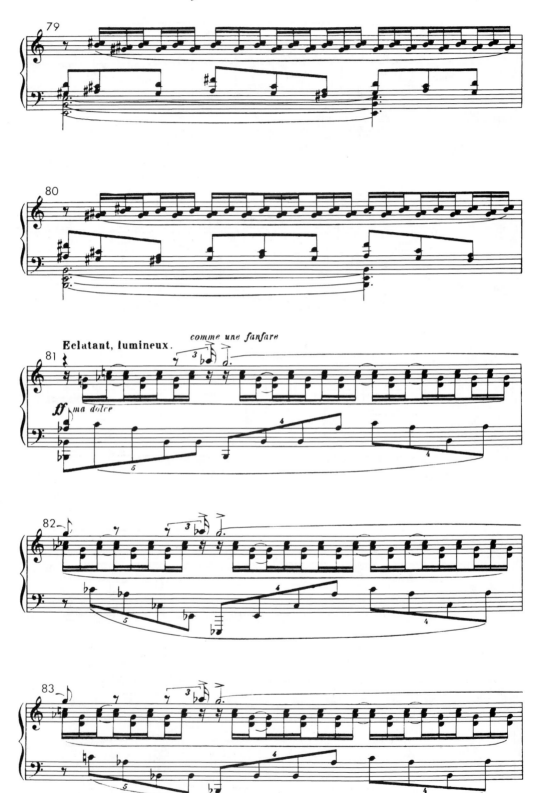

This piece for piano, dating from 1914, exploits both tertial and quartal combinations as well as mixtures of the two. Interlocking tritones, as in the chord B♭-E-D-A♭, dominate the first part of the composition. Later in the introduction a third is added to this configuration. Rhythmically the introduction is quite amorphous. The succeeding sections are static harmonically without any sense of forward propulsion, but each possesses a consistent rhythmic profile, sometimes involving complex relationships between the hands, such as 9 against 5 or 4.

130   GABRIEL FAURÉ (1845–1924)

La bonne chanson, Op. 61

No. 6, *Avant que tu ne t'en ailles*

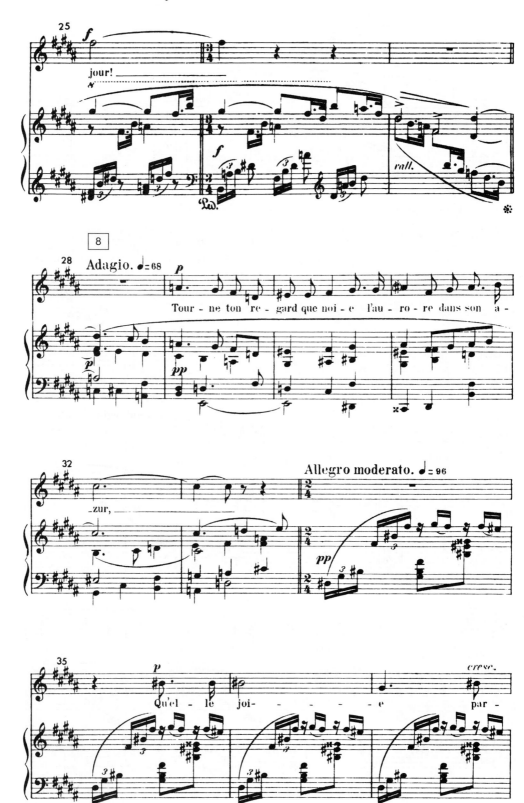

Avant que tu ne t'en ailles,
Pâle étoile du matin,
      —Mille cailles
Chantent, chantent dans le thym.—

Tourne devers le poète,
Dont les yeux sont pleins d'amour.
      —L'alouette
Monte au ciel avec le jour.—

Tourne ton regard que noie
L'aurore dans son azur;
      —Quelle joie
parmi les champs de blé mûr!—

Et fais luire ma pensée
Là-bas,—bien loin, oh! bien loin!
      —La rosée
Gaîment, brille sur le foin.—

Before you go,
Pale star of the morning,
      —a thousand quails
sing, sing in the thyme.—

Turn toward the poet,
whose eyes are filled with love.
      —The lark
climbs to the sky with the day.—

Turn your gaze that the dawn
drowns in its sky-blue tint.
      —What joy
in the fields of ripe wheat!—

Make glisten my thought
down there—quite far, o, quite far!
      —The dew
merrily sparkles on the hay.—

Dans le doux rêve où s'agite	In the sweet dream in which stirs
Ma vie endormie encor . . .	My life, still asleep . . .
—Vite, vite,	—Quick, quick,
Car voici le soleil d'or.—	for here is the golden sun.—

—PAUL VERLAINE

For *La bonne chanson* (1892) Fauré arranged poems of Paul Verlaine (1844–1896) to relate a story and used recurrent musical themes to unify the cycle. In this song, fragmentary phrases of melody, one for each verse, decline to commit their allegiance to any major or minor scale. The uncertain tonality, which has been attributed to Fauré's schooling in the modal idiom of plainchant, derives partly from his lowering of the leading tone. The harmony, thus shielded from the pull of the tonic, and further deprived of tension and resolution by the introduction of foreign notes that neutralize the chords' tendencies, achieves an equilibrium and repose that is the antithesis of the emotional unrest in Wagner's music. For example, the chords in measures 37–41 consist mainly of dominant sevenths and ninths, but the tension melts as one chord fades into another and the dissonant seventh or ninth that demanded resolution becomes a wayward member of another chord.

This style suits the shifting moods of Verlaine's poem. In the first half of each stanza the lover laments the fading of the morning star and the dawn that will wake his sleeping mate, while in the second halves he rejoices at the signs of day—the call of the quail and skylark, the stirring of the ripe wheat, and the dew sparkling on the hay. For the first lines, Fauré preferred a modal melody, tinged with segments of the whole-tone scale (for example, measures 16–19), dark meandering harmonies, subdued accompaniment, and slow motion; for the second halves he chose major chords, clear but static harmonies, and animated independent accompaniment. Thus the music, like the poem, juxtaposes vague subjective moods with vivid impressions of nature.

CLAUDE DEBUSSY (1862–1918)

Trois Nocturnes

Nuages

Reprinted from Debussy, *Nocturnes* (New York: Kalmus, n.d.), pp. 2–18.

The *Nocturnes* (1899) consist of three orchestral images: *Nuages* (Clouds), *Fêtes* (Festivals), and *Sirènes* (Sirens), in the last of which a wordless chorus of women's voices is added to the orchestra. *Nuages* begins with a chordal pattern borrowed from Musorgsky's song *Okonchen prazdnyi, shumnyi den'* (The idle, noisy day is over, NAWM 128), but where Musorgsky alternated sixths and thirds, Debussy used the starker-sounding fifths and thirds. As in the Musorgsky model there is an impression of movement but no harmonic direction, a perfect analogy for slowly moving clouds. Against this background a fragmentary English-horn melody tracing a tritone and soft French-horn calls on the same interval pierce the mist.

To connect disparate segments of the piece, Debussy twice used descending parallel chords, notably consecutive ninth chords (measure 61). It is evident that, as in works by Musorgsky and Fauré, chords are not used to shape a phrase by tension and release. Instead, each chord is conceived as a sonorous unit in a phrase whose structure is determined more by melodic shape or color value than by the movement of the harmony. Such a procedure does not negate tonality, which Debussy maintained in this piece by pedal points or frequent returns to the primary chords of the key.

The middle section of *Nuages*—the piece is in the ABA form Debussy favored—has a more exotic source. Debussy heard a *gamelan,* a Javanese orchestra made up mainly of gongs and percussion, at the Paris Exposition in 1889. He simulated the *gamelan* texture by giving the flute and harp a simple pentatonic tune, analogous to the Javanese nuclear theme, while the other instruments supply a static background (which, however, only occasionally approaches the colotomic method of the Javanese players, who enter in a predetermined staggered order). The return of the A section is fragmentary, like a dream imperfectly recollected.

MAURICE RAVEL (1875–1937)

Le Tombeau de Couperin

Menuet

In the suite from which this minuet is taken, Ravel paid tribute to François Couperin in the manner of the seventeenth-century *tombeaux,* which, however, were allemandes rather than suites of pieces such as this one (see Froberger's *Lamentation* in NAWM 67). Originally written for piano during the years 1914–17, the suite consisted of movements titled *Prélude, Fugue, Forlane, Rigaudon, Menuet,* and *Toccata.* Ravel arranged it for orchestra in 1919, omitting the fugue and toccata.

The melody is clearly phrased in groups of four measures, with a tonic cadence at the end of the first phrase and a mediant cadence with raised third at the end of the second. The second half of the binary dance form, following the archaic practice, begins on the dominant and proceeds to the tonic. The trio is in the parallel minor. This classic simplicity of musical form contrasts with the highly refined use of the orchestra, strings constantly changing from arco to pizzicato, or from unison to divisi, not to mention special effects such as harmonics and muted passages. Mutes also mask the color of the horns and trumpets; the result, however, is not the shifting veils of impressionism but the delineation of blocks of phrases and the silhouetting of contrapuntal lines, a transparency that recalls Mozart more than Couperin. The many drones remind one of the latter's imitations of the bagpipe in his musettes.

Béla Bartók (1881–1945)

Music for Strings, Percussion, and Celesta

Adagio (third movement)

*) *Griffbezeichnung* / indique la manière de toucher

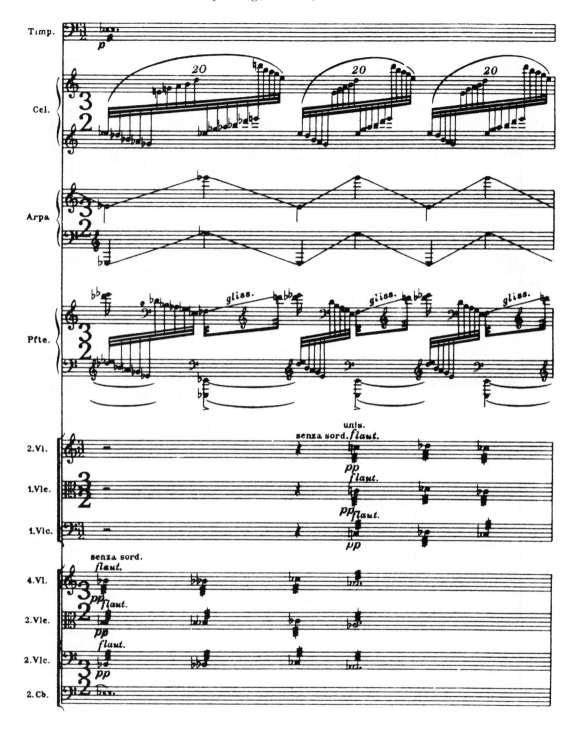

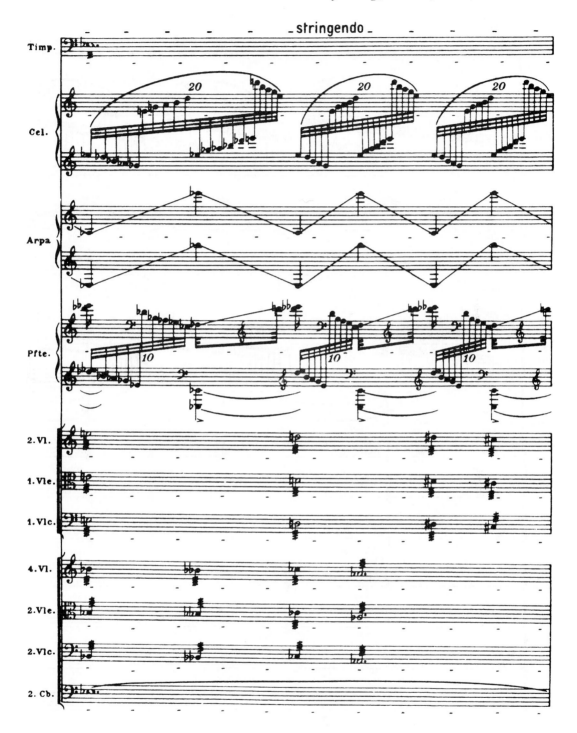

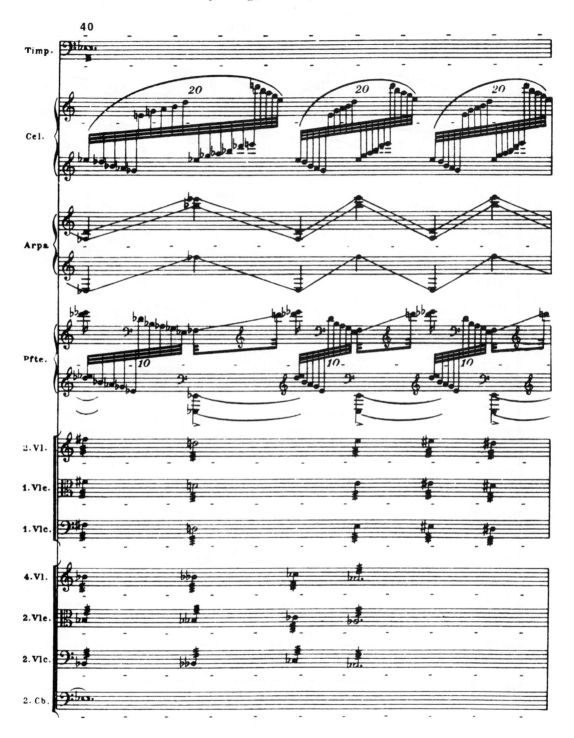

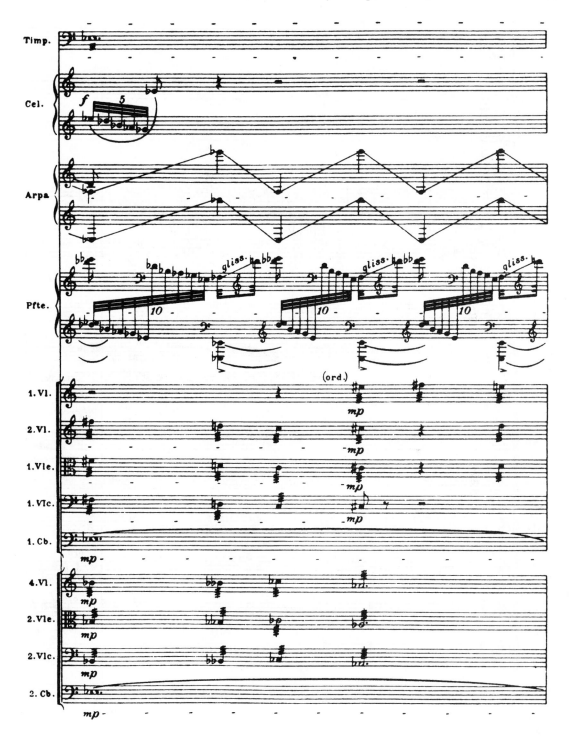

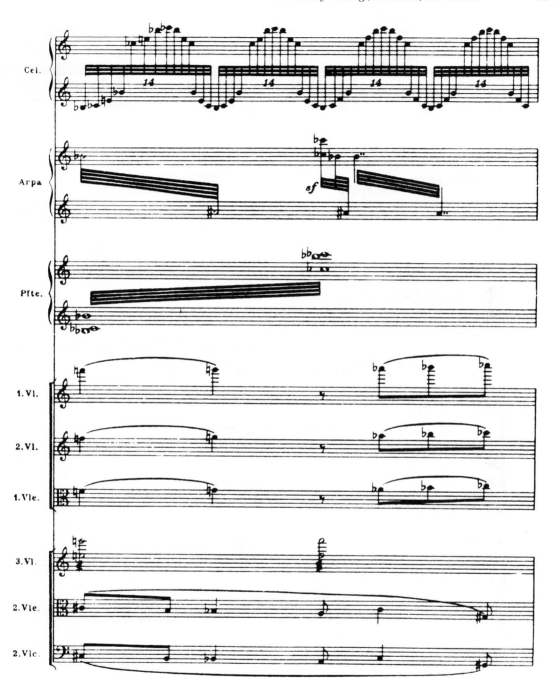

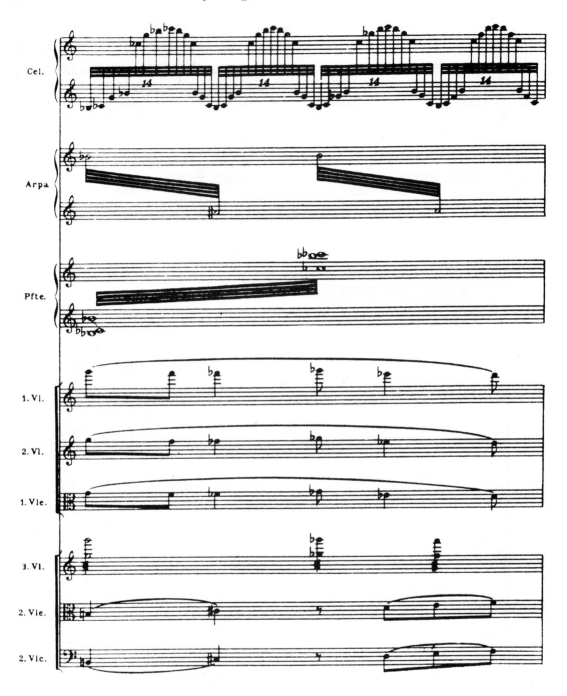

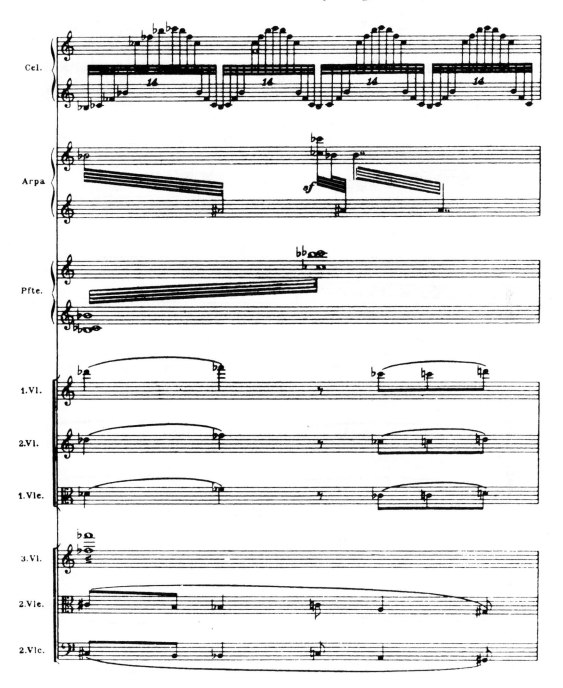

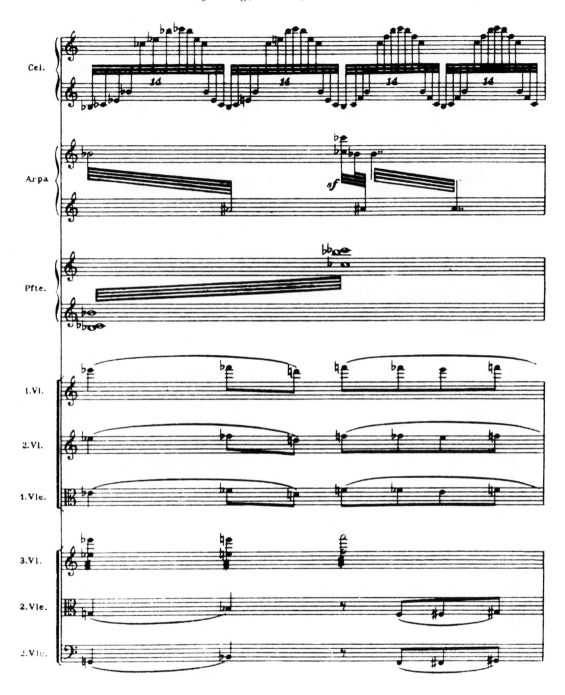

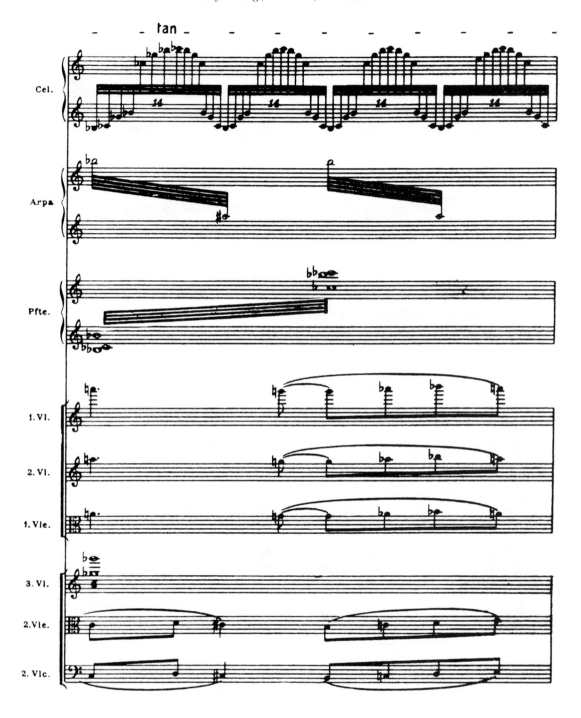

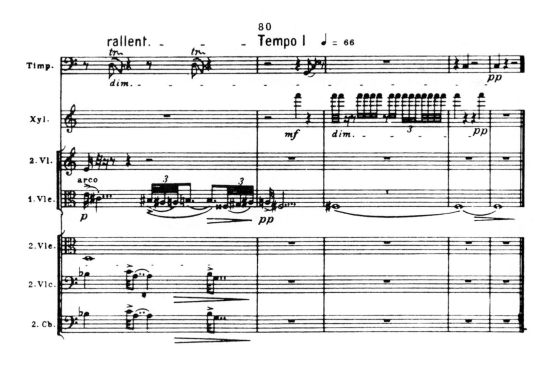

In this chamber work of 1936, Bartók experimented with mirror form on both a minute and a large scale. The opening xylophone solo of the Adagio displays it in microcosm: from the midpoint at the beginning of measure 3, the rhythm is identical going in either direction. On a larger scale, at the middle of the piece, measures 49–50 are essentially a retrograde of measures 47–48. This is also the midpoint of the formal scheme of the movement: Prologue ABCDCBA Epilogue.

Several diverse styles may be discerned. The A sections (measures 6–20 and 77–79) are in the *parlando-rubato* idiom of Serbo-Croatian folksong. (Compare the song of Example 20.4a in HWM with the first measures of the Adagio's A section.) The B section (measures 20–34), which recurs in combination with the C section, represents another folk technique, in which instruments play in octaves against drones and a chordal tapestry of sound is produced by plucked instruments. The resulting sound textures may be heard in music played by Bulgarian dance orchestras. Bartók here also adopted the Bulgarian dance rhythm of 2 + 3 + 3.

The C sections (measures 35–44 and 65–74) are examples of what has come to be known as Bartók's "night music" because of its association with the movement *Musiques nocturnes* in his expressionistic piano suite *Out of Doors* (1926). Two mutually exclusive pentatonic scales are juxtaposed in figurations played by the celesta and piano. The D section, which includes the mirror writing, is again made up of drones and octave doublings (measures 45–64). In this Adagio, then, Bartók has fully assimilated styles of improvised folk music into one of his most original and thoroughly deliberated works of art music.

Sofia Gubaidulina (b. 1931)

Rejoice! Sonata for Violin and Violoncello

Listen to the still small voice within (fifth movement)

Edition Sikorski H.S.1872, copyright 1990 by Musikverlag Hans Sikorski, Hamburg; 1992 assigned to Musikverlag Hans Sikorski, Hamburg, for entire world except C.I.S.

This composition is a study in chromatics, glissandos, tremolos, and harmonics. It was written in 1981 and first performed in Kuhmo, Finland, in
1988. The quotations heading the movements are from the spiritual lessons
of the Ukrainian philosopher Grigory Skovoroda (1722–1794). According
to the composer, the theme of *Rejoice* is represented

> as a metaphor for the transition into an "other" reality through the
> juxtaposition of normal sound with that of harmonics. The possibility
> for string instruments to derive pitches of various heights at one and
> the same place on the string can be experienced in music as the tran-
> sition to another plane of existence. And that is joy. Of course, the
> sounds of harmonics have been used a thousand times, and there is
> nothing special in it. But the idea is to experience them not as timbre
> or coloration, not as the trappings of the thing but as its essence, the
> essence of its form, as "transfiguration." And that is a matter of art.*

There are two main alternating textures in this movement: sixteenth-
note figuration in the violin against a slow-moving line in the cello; and
pizzicato leaps and double and triple stops in the violin against static notes
in the cello. In the first of these textures, both the violin and the cello move
in semitones and whole tones around a focal point. In the case of the violin,
this focus rises by half steps until it reaches the *B♭* an octave above the staff,
at which point the second texture begins and releases the tension. In a third
texture, which occurs only once, the violin plays rising and descending diatonic major scales against sustained notes in the cello. At the end, fulfilling
the allegory mentioned by the composer of reaching for joy, the cello plays
a series of glissandos from low fundamental tones to high artificial harmonics. The piece ends in a high F♯-major triad made up of natural harmonics.

*Quoted by Laurel Fay in liner notes for CD recording CBS MK 44924 (1985).

Dmitri Shostakovich (1906–1975)

Lady Macbeth of the Mtsensk District, Op. 29

Act IV: Final scene (excerpt): *Vot yésli gdye-nibúd'*

Musikverlag Hans Sikorski. G. Schirmer U.S. sole representative. Translation by Edward Downes.

(Katerina sees what is happening and rushes after Sergei

Kat.

Son.

Ser - gei, _____ Ser - gei,

What   a [brute!]
                  [man!]

p cresc.

but the female convicts hold her back and start jeering at her.)

Kat.

My stock - ings— you want them for Son-yet - ka? Ser - gei! Ser -

Kat.

gei! _____ A WOMAN CONVICT *ff marcato*

Now the merchant's wife's a -

Chorus of Female Convicts

S

Ha - ha-ha - ha-ha-ha - ha - ha - ha-ha-ha - ha!

A

Woman Convict: flame, she wants her lov-er, but her lov-er has grown cold and he

517

W. Con.: doesn't want to know her!

S Chorus: But her lov-er has grown cold, and he doesn't want to know her! Ha-

A

W. Con.: That's the end of it for Kat-ya; First of all she lost her

S Chorus: ha-ha-ha-ha - ha!

A

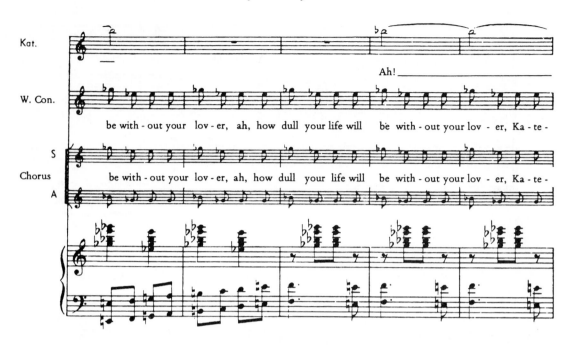

Guard: Quiet____ there!   Quiet_____ there!   What's all the yel-ling?

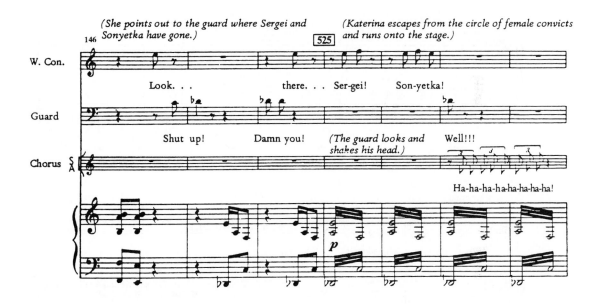

(She points out to the guard where Sergei and Sonyetka have gone.) **146** **525** *(Katerina escapes from the circle of female convicts and runs onto the stage.)*

W. Con.: Look. . .   there. . . Ser-gei!   Son-yetka!

Guard: Shut up!   Damn you!   *(The guard looks and shakes his head.)*   Well!!!

Chorus S/A: Ha-ha-ha-ha-ha-ha-ha-ha!

(Katerina stands motionless in an attitude of utter despair.)

Guard: I'll be damned!

Chorus S/A: Ha - ha - ha-ha-ha!

35 *(Katerina rushes in horror to the front of the stage—then stands once more in utter despair.)*

KATERINA

I know a lake in the forest,   far, far a-way;   the lake's

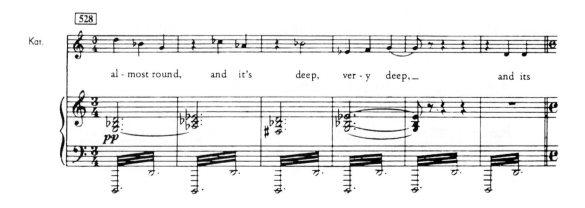

al - most round,   and it's   deep,   ver - y deep,—   and its

wa - ters are grim and black, grim and black __ like my con - science.

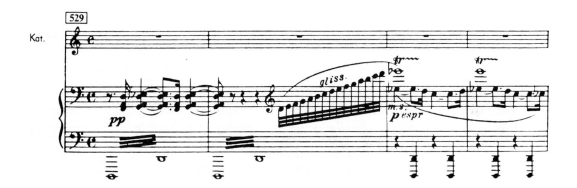

When the wind howls its way through the woods the

dark wa - ters rise in ter - ri - ble an - ger, __ e - nor-mous

(This scene takes place in Siberia on the banks of a river. The convicts are settling down for the night. Women are separated from men. Guards are posted everywhere.)

SERGEI

Vot yésli gdye-nibúd'	If only I could get hold
Sherstyanyye chulki dostát'	of some woolen stockings somewhere.
Pomogló b navyeérno!	That would surely help.

KATERINA

Chulki?	Stockings?
Shto zhe ty ránshe molchál?	Why didn't you mention it before,
Seryozha? Na chulki, vozmi chulki!	Seryozha? Here, take these.

(She takes off her stockings)

SERGEI

Akh, Kátya,	Oh Katya,
Spasibo, rádost' ty moyá!	thank you. You're a darling.

KATERINA *(giving him her stockings)*

Vot, vozmi.	Here, take them.

SERGEI

Nu, ya seychás pridú!   Well, I'll be back right away.

(He grabs the stockings and starts quickly towards Sonyetka)

KATERINA

Kudá ty?   Where are you going?

SERGEI

Seychás pridú.   I'll be back in a moment.

KATERINA

Seryozha, Seryozha!   Seryozha, Seryozha!
Zachém on ushól?   Why has he left?

SERGEI *(to Sonyetka)*

Na chulki!   Here are some stockings.
Idyóm, tepyér ty moyá!   Come, now you are mine!

(He takes Sonyetka in his arms and carries her offstage)

SONYETKA *(delighted)*

Ish, zvyer!   You're a beast!

*(Katerina observes what is going on and rushes after Sergei,
but the other women convicts restrain and mock her)*

KATERINA

Sergéy, Sergéy, shto éto?   Sergei, Sergei, what's going on?
Chulki Sonyétke?   The stockings are for Sonyetka?
Sergei, Sergei!   Sérgey, Sérgey!

WOMEN CONVICTS

Ha, ha, ha . . . !   Ha, ha, ha . . . !

WOMAN CONVICT

U kupchikhi zhar i pyl!   The merchant's wife's passion
Yeshchó klokóchut.   still burns
A lyubóvnichek ostyl,   but her lover's has cooled —
On i znat´ yeyó nye khóchet!   he has no desire to know her.

WOMEN CONVICTS

A lyubóvnichek ostyl,   Her lover's passion has cooled —
On i znat´ yeyó nye khóchet!   he has no desire to know her.
Ha, ha, ha . . . !   Ha, ha, ha . . . !

WOMAN CONVICT

Nichevó nye stálo bóle: She has nothing left:
Poteryála svoi rádosti na vóle!   she lost her wealth and freedom,
A v nevóle zhenikhá!   and her new husband too.

WOMEN CONVICTS

Ha, ha, ha . . . !	Ha, ha, ha . . . !
Poteryála svoi rádosti na vóle!	She lost her wealth and freedom,
A v nevóle zhenikhá!	and her new husband too.

WOMAN CONVICT

Katerina Lvóvna,	Katerina Lvovna,
Natvorila ty delóv!	what a mess you've made of your life!

WOMAN CONVICT

Byez Sergéya Katerine óchen skúshno!	Your life will be dull without Sergei.

WOMEN CONVICTS

Kupchikha byez Sergéya propadyót	The merchant's wife will be lost without Sergei.
Byez Sergéya Katerine óchen skúshno!	Your life will be dull without Sergei.

WOMAN CONVICT

Otdáy, Otdáy, Otdáy, chúlochki nam!	Let's have the stockings back.

WOMEN CONVICTS

Ha, ha, ha . . . !	Ha, ha, ha . . . !
Otdáy chúlochki nam!	Let's have the stockings back.

KATERINA *(still trying to break through the women convicts)*

Akh! Pustíte!	Ah! Let me go!

WOMAN CONVICT

Ni odnú nye spitsa nóchku . . .	She won't sleep a wink at night . . .
Nepriyátno v odinóchku.	She'll be miserable and lonely.
Nepriyátno byez Sergéya!	She'll be lost without Sergei.

WOMEN CONVICTS

Ha, ha, ha . . . !	Ha, ha, ha . . . !

KATRINA

Akh! Akh!	Ah! Ah!

ALL WOMEN CONVICTS

Byez Sergéya Katerine óchen skúshno.	Without Sergei life will be dull.
Byez Sergéya Katerine óchen skúshno.	Without Sergei life will be dull.
Byez Sergéya Katerine óchen skúshno.	Without Sergei life will be dull.
Byez Sergéya.	Without Sergei.

GUARD *(hearing the noise, comes running, restores order)*

Smirno! Smirno!	Attention! Attention!
Chevú oryóte?	What's all the shouting?

WOMAN CONVICT (*points out to the guard where Sonyetka and Sergei have gone*)

Tam . . . tam . . . Sergéy, Sonyétka.

There . . . there . . . Sergei, Sonyetka

GUARD

Molchát′ Ya vas!

Shut up! Damn you!

(*He looks and shakes his head*)

Nu!

Well!

(*Katerina breaks away from the women convicts and runs onto the stage*)

WOMEN CONVICTS

Ha, ha, ha . . . !

Ha, ha, ha . . . !

GUARD

Nu i nu!

I'll be damned!

WOMEN CONVICTS

Ha, ha, ha . . . !

Ha, ha, ha . . . !

(*Katerina, in utter despair, stands motionless, then rushes in horror
to the front of the stage, where she stands once more in utter despair*)

KATERINA

V iesú, v sámoy cháshche yest′ ózero,
Sovsyém krúgloe, óchen glubókoe,
I vodá v nyom chórnaya,
Kak moyá sóvest′, chórnaya.
I kogdá vyéter khódit v iesú,
Na ózere podnimáyutsa vólny,
Bol′shíe vólny, togdá stráshno;
A ósenyu v ózere vsegdá vólny,
Chórnaya vodá i bol′shie vólny
Chórnyye bol′shie vólny.

In a forest, far away, there is a lake.
It is almost round and very deep.
Its waters are black,
as my conscience is black.
and when the wind blows in the woods,
on the lake the waves rise up,
huge waves that inspire terror.
In the fall on the lake the waves swell—
black water and enormous waves,
huge black waves.

(*Sonyetka and Sergei return from backstage*)

SERGEI

Znáesh li, Sonyétka
Na kovó s tobóy my pokhózhi?
Na Adáma i na Evu.

Do you know, Sonyetka,
whom we resemble?
Adam and Eve.

SONYETKA

No na ray zdyes nye slishkom-to pokhózhe!

But it doesn't look much like Paradise.

SERGEI

Pustyaki, mi seychás pobyváli v rayú.

Nonsense, we have just been together in Paradise.

SONYETKA *(going up to Katerina, who sits motionless, her eyes fixed on one spot)*

Spasíbo, Katerina Lvóvna.	Thank you, Katerina Lvovna,
Spasíbo, Katerina Lvóvna.	Thank you, Katerina Lvovna,
Za chulki spasíbo!	for the stockings, thank you.
Posmotri, kak krasívo	Look how becoming
Na moíkh nogákh sidyát.	they are on my legs.
Seryózha mnye ikh nadevál	Seryozha put them on for me
I nógi potselúyami mnye sogrevál.	after kissing my legs to warm them up.
Akh Serózha, moy Seryózha,	Oh, Seryozha, my Seryozha,
Katerina dúra,	Katerina is a fool,
Nye sumyéla uderzhát' Sergéya.	because she couldn't hold on to Sergei.
Ekh, dúra! Ekh, dúra!	Ha, what a fool! What a fool!
A chúlochki nye vidát',	And you won't see your stockings again.
Oni tepyér moi, vidish?	They now belong to me; look!
Mnye tepyér tepló!	Now I'm warm.

Shostakovich completed the original version of this four-act opera in 1932. The libretto, by the composer and Alexander Preis, is based on a short story by Nikolai Leskov (1831–1895) about a small-town Lady Macbeth. The opera was first performed at the Maly Opera Theater in Leningrad (now St. Petersburg) on January 22, 1934. Shostakovich called the opera a tragedy-satire. He treated the heroine, Katerina Izmailova ("Lady Macbeth"), wife of a provincial merchant, sympathetically as a tragic victim. Her wimpish husband, her autocratic and lustful father-in-law, the police, the prisoners' guards, and her greedy, vulgarly suave seducer Sergei, who becomes her lover—these parts he wrote as musical caricatures. Katerina, unhappy and unfulfilled in her marriage, murders her husband with the encouragement and help of Sergei and hides the body, then proceeds to marry her lover in a sumptuous wedding. Their crime is soon discovered, and they are sentenced and forced to march to Siberia with other prisoners.

The opera gained immediate success—it received nearly 200 performances in Moscow and Leningrad and was staged in many cities, including Cleveland, New York, and Philadelphia. However in 1936, Stalin and a delegation of government officials were visibly displeased when they saw the opera, walking out before it was over. Two days later the work was denounced in *Pravda,* the Communist Party newspaper:

> Listeners were stunned by a flood of intentionally discordant sounds. Scraps of melody, fragmentary musical phrases rise to the surface but are then drowned in the mass, escape for a moment, and are lost again in the gnashing, screeching din. It is difficult to follow this music; it is impossible to enjoy it. . . . The capacity of good music to capture the public is sacrificed at the altar of petty-bourgeois formalism. . . . The danger of such an orientation for Soviet music is obvious. . . . While our critics embrace the ideal of Socialist Realism, our musical stage presents, in the opera of Shostakovich, the coarsest naturalism.

The "review" devastated the composer and sent shock waves through the Soviet music world. It was in effect an unsigned editorial that marked the imposition of rigid Soviet state control over cultural policy and the arts. The opera soon ceased to be performed. Ten years after Stalin died, a revised version, Op. 114, was produced in Moscow in 1963 as *Katerina Izmailova*. The composer, who had toned down some of the vulgar language and erotic allusions, which some had called "pornophonic", considered this version an improvement in both text and music. However, the excerpt of the score and libretto reprinted here is from the original version, which is that used in most recent performances, including the revival at the Metropolitan Opera in New York in 1995.

The final scene takes place on the banks of a river, where the convicts pause in their march to Siberia. As the prisoners settle down for the night, Sergei, who bribes a guide to get to the women's quarters, smooth-talks a pretty fellow-convict, Sonyetka, into a love tryst in a dark corner; he has bought her compliance with a pair of wool stockings, which he convinced Katerina to sacrifice by pretending that he could not survive the cold without them. At the end Katerina jumps into the river in despair, dragging Sonyetka with her, and both drown in the swift current.

The music, as in most post-Wagnerian opera, is continuous, without distinct recitatives and arias. But a number of monologues, duets, and choral scenes are unified by texture, rhythmic figures, orchestration, and tonal devices.

The excerpt begins with a persistent rhythm in a solo drum (represented by repeated semitone cluster *E-F* in the piano reduction at 1 measure after No. 510), followed by some ironic commentary by the woodwinds as Sergei begs Katerina for her wool stockings. The scene that includes the exchange of warm leggings is punctuated by the jeering measured laughter of the chorus of women convicts. Honeyed harmonies and sequences expose Sergei's phony sentimentality as he thanks his wife for the stockings (2 measures before No. 513).

Katerina, brooding on her "black conscience" (Nos. 526 to 533), hallucinates in a passage characterized by an unstable Phrygian mode and shifting meters; she is accompanied by an expressionistic orchestration entirely on a *D* pedal dominated by the timpani. Sergei's dialogue with Sonyetka after their fling (Nos. 534 to 536) parodies Italian opera with its oom-pah accompaniment, the expansive chromatic lyricism of a flute obbligato, and tonic-dominant harmonies. Sonyetka scornfully flaunts her victory over Katerina (Nos. 536 to 540) in music of a more varied texture organized around the note *G* and culminating in a series of mock-Wagnerian sequences.

Where the Stalinist cultural watchdogs heard abrasive dissonances and an incoherent din, we hear a prevailing diatonicism in both the vocal lines and the accompaniment. But the frequent defiance of functional harmony and the dynamic scoring supporting the bustling stage action keep audience members at the edge of their seats.

Paul Hindemith (1895–1963)

Mathis der Maler

Sechstes Bild

38

Very slow, free in measure
Sehr langsam, frei im Zeitmaß

Vorhang auf · Curtain

SIXTH TABLEAU

The Odenwald. A region with tall trees in the late twilight.
Regina rushes in, Mathis close behind her.

MATHIS

Du wirst mich verlieren. Es is zu lange her,
Daß ich so jung war wie du und so schnell.

You almost lost me. It was too long ago
that I was as young and as fast as you.

REGINA
(in feverish haste)

Laß uns doch
Weiterlaufen.

Let us then
go on.

MATHIS

Wohin willst du in der Nacht?

Where would you go in the dark?

REGINA

Wer   Who could

Hat mir je gesagt, wohin der Weg geht? Noch   ever tell me where the path leads? Yet
Immer drangen wir ins Unbekannte.   we always hurry into the unknown.

MATHIS

Keiner jagt   No one chases

Uns mehr.   us any more.

REGINA

Wie weißt du das? Der liebste   How do you know that? My dearest
  Vater, er verstand   father—he understood
Mich ohne Worte, er führte mich zart an der Hand. me without words; he led me tenderly by the hand.
Und nur einmal, zuletzt, ließ er   And only once, for the last time, did he
Mich allein zurück. Seit ich ihn tot liegen sah,   leave me behind alone. For then I saw him lying dead
In Blute, mit offnen Augen, die wie ein   in blood, with eyes open, as if
Wunder des Himmels Schwärze anstarrten, mit den he were staring at the mystery of heaven's darkness,
  angstvoll   his pained
Verkrallten Händen, schüttelt mich die Angst, daß der hands twisted. I tremble with anxiety for fear that
Tote Mann mir folgt. Er holt mich ein,   the dead man is following me. He is overtaking me,
  ist nah,   he is nearby.
Ergreift mich. Und wie sehnlich wünschte ich, mein He grabs me. How ardently I wish that
Herz bei ihm in Ruhe zu betten. Soll mich   he would put my heart to rest. Shall the
  Sehnsucht, soll   longing
Mich Entsetzen lähmen? Sage mir: wo ist er?   and fear cripple me? Tell me, where is he?
Versinkt ein Toter, wird es erhoben?   A dead man sinks down; will he be lifted up?
Laß mich nicht allein!   Do not leave me alone.

MATHIS

Mein Töchterlein, zusammen bleiben wir.   My little girl, we shall remain together.

(He kisses her)

Beruhige dich. Lege dich zum Schlaf auf meinem Now have a rest. Lie down to sleep on my
Mantel.   cloak.

(He spreads out his cloak for her to lie on, beds her down and sits next to her comfortingly)

Wie mürbe ist des Alters Pein,   How weary is the pain of old age,
Maßlos das Leid der Jugend.—Alte Märchen woben boundless the sorrow of youth!—Old tales they wove:
Uns fromme Bilder, die in Widerscheinen   to us innocent images that are a reflection
Das Höheren sind. Ihr Sinn ist dir   of higher things. Their sense
Fern, du kannst ihn nur erahnen.   eludes you; you can only surmise it.
Und frömmer noch reden   And more uncannily still do tones speak
Zu uns die Töne, wenn Musik, in Einfalt hier   to us when music strikes up,
Geboren, die Spur himmlischer Herkunft trägt.   bearing a sign of heavenly origin.
Sieh, wie eine Schar von Engeln ewige   See how a troop of angels wanders through eternal
  Bahnen   paths
In irdischen Wegen abwandelt. Wie spürt man jeden in an earthly direction. See how each one
Versenkt in sein mildes Amt. Der eine geigt   is absorbed in his tender task! One fiddles:
Mit wundersam gesperrtem Arm, den Bogen   with wonderfully outstretched arm, he balances the
  wägt   bow.

Er zart, damit nicht eines wenigen Schattens Rauheit	He fondles it so that not a shadow of coarseness
Den linden Lauf trübe. Ein andrer streicht	disturbs its gentle course. Another strokes
Gehobnen Blicks aus Saiten seine Freude.	uplifted glances from the strings of his joy.
Verhaftet scheint der dritte dem fernen Geläute	A third seems to listen to the ringing of bells
Seiner Seele und achtet leicht des Spiels. Wie bereit	within his soul. How ready
Er ist, zugleich zu hören und zu dienen.	he is, both to hear and to serve.

REGINA

Es sungen drei Engel ein süßen Gesang,	Three angels sang a sweet song
Der weit in den hohen Himmel erklang.	that resounded widely through high heaven.

MATHIS

Ihr Kleid selbst musiziert mit ihnen.	Even their garments make music
In schillernden Federn schwirrt der Töne Gegenspiel.	as their iridescent feathers whir a countervoice.
Ein leichter Panzer unirdischen Metalls erglüht,	A light coat of mail of unearthly metal glows,
Berührt vom Wogen des Klanges wie vom Beben	shimmering with the waves of sound as with the trembling
Bewegten Herzens. Und im Zusammenklang viel	of an agitated heart. And through the harmony
Bunter Lichterkreise wird aus kaum gehörtem Lied	of countless bursts of color will form from a barely heard song
Auf wunderbare Art sichtbares Formenleben.	a wonderful kind of visible living form.

REGINA

Es eint sich mit ihnen der himmlische Chor,	Joining with them is the heavenly choir.
Sie singen Gott und den Heiligen vor.	They sing to God and the saints.

MATHIS
(Night has fallen)

Wie diese ihr klingendes Werk verrichten,	While some attend to their sonorous duties.
So beten andre. Mit weichen Füßen treten	others pray. With fleet feet they
Sie auf die weicheren Stufen der Töne. Und du.	descend the delicate steps of tones. And you
Weißt nicht: musizieren, die Gebete dichten	do not know whether, making music, they invent prayers
Oder hörst du der Musikanten Beten.	or whether you hear the musicians praying.
Ist so Musik Gebet geworden, hört lauschend zu	Has music, then, become prayer, as it imitates the harmony
Natur. Ein Rest des Schimmers solcher Sphären	of nature. A residue of splendor of those spheres
Mög unser dunkles Tun verklären.	may brighten up our dark path.

REGINA
(Falling asleep)

Die Welt is erfüllt von göttlichem Schall,	The world is filled with a godly ringing.
Im Herzen der Menschen ein Widerhall.	In the hearts of men sounds the echo.

—PAUL HINDEMITH

Hindemith wrote the opera *Mathis der Maler* on his own libretto during the years 1934–35, but it was not performed until 1938 in Zurich. The *Mathis der Maler* Symphony, containing earlier versions of the preludes to each of the opera's three acts, was first performed in Berlin in 1934. The subject of the opera is Matthias Grünewald, the painter of the famous Isenheim altarpiece, which consists of multiple painted panels (now in the museum in Colmar, Alsace, France). The painter is moved by the plight of the common people to leave his studio and join the Peasants' Revolt of 1524, but he eventually decides to renounce political action and return to his art.

The sixth scene demonstrates Hindemith's power to evoke the intensity of feeling behind the painter's creation of his polyptych and his deep commitment to the rights of the oppressed German people. The prelude to this scene is played before a closed curtain and is heard again later when Mathis, in despair over the defeat of the peasants, is tormented by visions resembling those in one of the panels of the altarpiece, *The Temptation of Saint Anthony.* By the first beat of the fourth measure, every tone of the chromatic scale has been stated at least once, as if it were to be a twelve-tone composition; it is not, though the restless, tortured line of the melody is a fine example of German expressionism. (This scene corresponds to the third movement of the symphony.)

Here, as elsewhere in the score, Hindemith followed a method he called "harmonic fluctuation." A passage begins with fairly consonant chords and progresses toward combinations containing greater tension and dissonance, which are then resolved either suddenly or by slowly moderating the tension until consonance is reached again. The method is also applied in the music that introduces Mathis's describing his vision of an angel concert to calm Regina, daughter of the slain chief of the Peasants' Army, whom he is leading to safety in the Odenwald forest (measure 198). Here Hindemith gives a musical representation of another of the paintings of the altarpiece, *The Angel Concert* (music that corresponds to the first movement of the symphony, see HWM, illustration opposite p. 750). Just before Regina falls asleep, the two sing the chorale *Es sungen drei Engel* (measure 320), adding to the already strong period atmosphere the fervor of the early years of the Reformation. (At the end of the opera, Mathis is reconciled to his role as artist by his patron, Cardinal Albrecht of Brandenburg, who appears to him in a vision as St. Paul converting Anthony and shows him that superior artistic endeavor is a worthy goal in itself.)

137 IGOR STRAVINSKY (1882–1971)

Le Sacre du printemps

Danse des adolescentes

164

The large number of Russian folksong quotations and folklike tunes employed in *Le Sacre* should have made the music quite palatable to the Parisian audience that first saw the ballet in 1913. But there were disturbing features of both the music and the scenario, which calls for an adolescent girl elected for sacrifice to dance herself to death. The most unusual passage is in the second scene, the *Danse des adolescentes* (Dance of the Adolescent Girls). The lower strings, divisi, play an E-major triad (spelled *Fb-Ab-Cb*) while the upper strings, also divisi, sound a first-inversion seventh chord on *Eb*. This collection of pitches approximates the octatonic scale, *Eb-E-(F♯)-G-A-Bb-C-Db-Eb*—a scale that alternates semitones and whole tones. This scale does not account, however, for the *Ab* or *Cb* that are heard in the unusual sonority.

The barring is regular but marked with an extraordinary pattern of syncopations and accents. The accented chords are reinforced by eight horns doubling the notes of the strings. The accents result in the following grouping of eighth notes: $9 + 2 + 6 + 3 + 4 + 5 + 3$ (=32). This destroys any feeling of metrical regularity, yet the passage forms an eight-measure period. Then for four measures the English horn plays a fragmentary melody with the three of the uppermost notes of the octatonic scale against arpeggios that spell out three complementary notes of that scale, though a foreign *B* again intrudes. Now the pounding chords resume, but leaving out the first four beats, so that the pattern becomes $5 + 2 + 6 + 3$ (=16) for another four-bar phrase. The passage is cleverly conceived for ballet, since the dancers can continue to count four-measure phrases while the spectator-listener is utterly disoriented metrically and rhythmically.

Later the three top notes of the chord—*Bb-Db-Eb*—are combined with five notes of the C-major scale to form another ostinato pattern against which a modal Russian tune is played in the French horn and flute (measure 89). This tune, heard in several keys over a variety of ostinatos, dominates the remainder of the excerpt.

138 ARNOLD SCHOENBERG (1874–1951)

Pierrot lunaire, Op. 21

Nos. 8 and 13

a) No. 8, *Nacht*

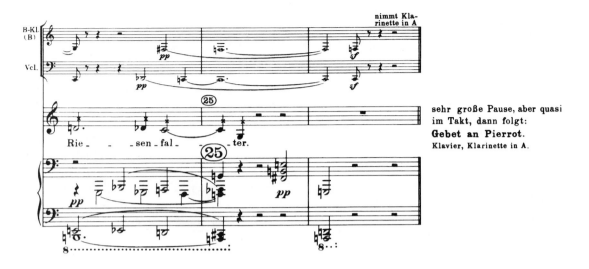

sehr große Pause, aber quasi
im Takt, dann folgt:
Gebet an Pierrot.
Klavier, Klarinette in A.

b) No. 13, *Enthauptung*

folgt: **Die Kreuze**
unmittelbar anschließend.
Klavier (anfangs allein) später
dazu Flöte,Klar.(A),Geige,Vell.

⌐ ⌐ bedeutet Hauptstimme.

NACHT

Finstre, schwarze Riesenfalter
Töteten der Sonne Glanz.
Ein geschloßnes Zauberbuch,
Ruht der Horizont—verschwiegen.

Aus dem Qualm verlorner Tiefen
Steigt ein Duft, Erinnrung mordend!
Finstre, schwarze Riesenfalter
Töteten der Sonne Glanz.

Und vom Himmel erdenwärts
Senken sich mit schweren Schwingen
Unsichtbar die Ungetüme
Auf die Menschenherzen nieder . . .
Finstre, schwarze Riesenfalter.

NIGHT

Gloomy, black bats
killed the radiant sun.
A sealed book of magic,
the horizon rests, taciturn.

From the vapor of forgotten depths
rises a fragrance, killing memory!
Gloomy, black bats
killed the radiant sun.

And from heaven earthwards
they sink with ponderous oscillations—
invisible, the monsters,
down to the hearts of men . . .
Gloomy, black bats.

ENTHAUPTUNG

Der Mond, ein blankes Türkenschwert,
Auf einen schwarzen Seidenkissen,
Gespenstisch groß—dräut er hinab
Durch schmerzensdunkle Nacht.

Pierrot irrt ohne Rast umber
Und starrt empor in Todesängsten
Zum Mond, dem blanken Türkenschwert
Auf einem schwarzen Seidenkissen.

Es schlottern unter ihm die Knie,
Ohnmächtig bricht er jäh zusammen.
Er wähnt: es sause strafend schon
Auf seinen Sündenhals hernieder
Der Mond, das blanke Türkenschwert.

—ALBERT GIRAUD, translated from
the French by O. ERICH HARTLEBEN

DECAPITATION

The moon, a polished scimitar
set on a black silken cushion,
ghostly vast, menaces downwards
through pain's dark night.

Pierrot wanders about, restless,
and stares on high in death-agony
at the moon, a polished scimitar
set on a black silken cushion.

His knees knock together under him,
swooning, he collapses abruptly.
He fancies: let it whistle punishingly
already down on his guilty neck,
the moon, the polished scimitar.

The full title of Schoenberg's cycle of songs, from which we have selected two, was "Three times seven poems from Albert Giraud's *Pierrot lunaire.*" Completed in 1912, the set was scored for a speaker and five musicians, some of whom doubled on a second instrument: flute (piccolo), clarinet (bass clarinet), violin (viola), cello, and piano. Schoenberg set a translation by O. Erich Hartleben. The voice throughout the cycle declaims the text in a so-called *Sprechstimme* (speaking voice), approximating the written pitches but keeping closely to the notated rhythm. For this effect Schoenberg used the sign ♩. Some of the pieces rely on constructive devices such as canons to assure unity, since they cannot depend on chord relationships within a tonality for this purpose.

In No. 8, *Nacht* (Night), Pierrot sees somber black bats casting gloom over the world, shutting out the sun. Schoenberg calls No. 8 a passacaglia, but it is an unusual one in that the unifying motive, a rising minor third followed by a descending major third, appears constantly in various note values throughout the parts of the texture. The ubiquitous ostinato is a fitting artistic distillation of Pierrot's obsession with the giant bats that enclose him in a fearful trap.

No. 13, *Enthauptung* (Beheading), shows another side of Schoenberg's music in the early teens. Thematic development is abandoned for what appears to the listener as anarchic improvisation subject only to the changing message of the text. Here Pierrot imagines that he is beheaded for his crimes by the moonbeam. The first five measures sum up the poem and include a cascade of notes—partially in a whole-tone scale—in the bass clarinet and viola depicting the sweep of the scimitar. The next ten measures evoke the atmosphere of the moonlit night and Pierrot scurrying to avoid the moonbeam. Augmented chords in the piano evoke the image of his knees knocking. The piece ends with the downward runs heard before, this time in the piano, while the other instruments play glissandos. An Epilogue recalls the music of No. 7, *Der kranke Mond* (The Sick Moon). Just as certain expressionist painters distorted representations of real objects to reflect their feelings about their surroundings and themselves (see illustration HWM, facing p. 751), so Schoenberg used exaggerated graphic images and speech inflections in this work to express the poet's inner feelings.

ARNOLD SCHOENBERG

Variationen für Orchester, Op. 31

Theme and Variation VI

a) Theme

b) Variation VI

Composed between 1926 and 1928, the *Variations* are generally acknowledged to be one of Schoenberg's finest works, a good example of blending
traditional procedures with the twelve-tone technique. After an introduction, in which the row is surrounded by a veil of mystery and mood of
expectation, a twenty-four-measure theme is presented. Four forms of the

twelve-note row (see example below) determine the pitch successions of the melodic subject in the cello, while the same four forms in reverse order supply the harmonic accompaniment to this melody. The subject is clearly laid out in motives employing groups of three to six notes of the row. These groups are given distinct rhythmic shape; Schoenberg then employed their rhythms with different pitches in the course of the theme, contributing to the overall cohesion of the work.

The example below shows the first half of the theme, with numbers to indicate the pitch order in the four forms of the row. The first three motives use up the row in its original state (P-0, the Principal [P] form at the original pitch, represented by 0, that is, zero half steps of transposition). The harmony for each of the motives is drawn from the same numbers of the row but in the Inversion (I) transposed up a major sixth to the ninth half step (I-9). As the first group of motives had 5, 4, and 3 different pitches respectively, the second group has the reverse, 3, 4, and 5 pitches. The melody is now drawn from the Retrograde (R) of the Inversion at the ninth half step (RI-9), which had previously furnished the accompaniment.

Forms of the Twelve-Tone Row, First Half of Theme

In the first variation the theme is still in the lower voices, while the other instruments develop its motives as well as new ones in an antiphonal manner. The second variation is contrapuntal and chamberlike, a solo violin and oboe having a canon on the inverted form of the theme, which is still recognizable because of the motives' rhythmic and intervallic shapes. The rhythmic character of the theme weakens in the five subsequent variations, while prominence is given to new motives drawn from the forms of the row. As the motives of the theme retire into the rhythmic anonymity of the row, the result resembles a passacaglia.

The sixth variation (b) shows to what extent the theme, now in the cello, is transformed (though still preserving the note groupings) and subordinated to other events. One such new idea is the motive first heard in the flute, English horn, and bassoon; it features two of the most prominent intervals of the subject—the semitone and tritone—and it is heard repeatedly in the texture in both its direct and inverted forms. Thus, despite the new twelve-tone technique and the highly systematic organization of the pitch realm, Schoenberg's Op. 31 does not depart radically from the syntax and unifying devices found in variations of the Baroque, Classic, and Romantic periods.

140 ALBAN BERG (1885–1935)

Wozzeck, Op. 7

Act III, Scene 3

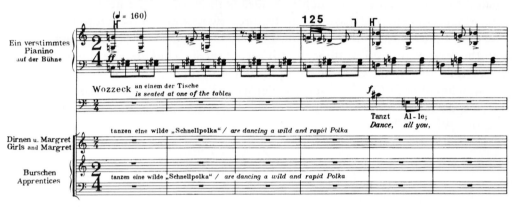

*) Triller ohne Nachschlag

plötzlich noch langsamer (♩ = 80)

Nein! kei-ne Schuh,   man kann auch bloß - fü-ßig   in die Höll'   geh'n!   Ich   möcht   heut
No! wear no shoes,   *one can go bare - foot-ed   down to hell*   *fire!*   *I   feel   like*

plötzlich noch langsamer (♩ = 80)

Alban Berg completed *Wozzeck* in 1922, and the opera received its first performance three years later in Berlin. Berg adapted the libretto from a play of the same name by Georg Büchner (1814–1837), which Berg saw in 1914 at its premiere in Vienna.

The music of this scene, a wild polka, is an invention on a rhythm. In the previous scene Wozzeck murdered his mistress, Marie, the mother of his child, because she had betrayed him with a fellow soldier, the Drum Major. Now Wozzeck sits in a cavern singing and drinking. He asks Margret, the barmaid, to dance with him; after they dance she sits on his lap and sings a song, during which she notices blood on his hand. He becomes agitated and obsessed with his blood.

In the first four measures a barroom piano announces in the right-hand part both the rhythmic theme and a set of six pitches, *G-E-A-F-E♭-D♭*. The pitch-set is one that recurs frequently in the opera; if listed in ascending or descending order, the pitches nearly form a whole-tone scale. The music of the scene is constructed like a medieval isorhythmic motet. A set of eight durations is continually reiterated, sometimes in diminution, sometimes in augmentation. It pervades the entire texture, even the voices. After Margret discovers the blood on Wozzeck's hands (measure 185) the two begin a canon on the rhythm, in which first the chorus (measure 202), then the instruments join. The harmony rises in a whole-tone succession of major sevenths (measures 187–207). Wozzeck's obsession with his guilt, symbolized in the persistent rhythm, shrieking dissonance, and the whole-tone scale formations, reaches an almost unbearable intensity.

141 ANTON WEBERN (1883–1945)

Symphonie, Op. 21

Ruhig schreitend (first movement)

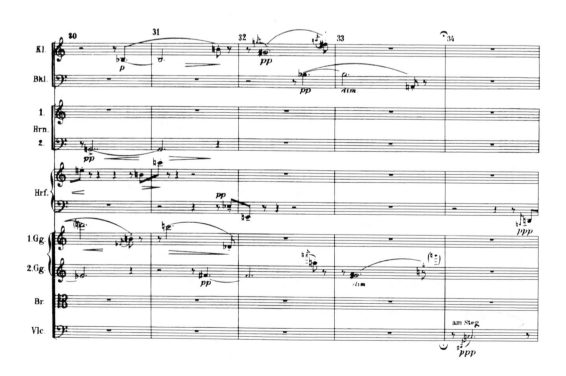

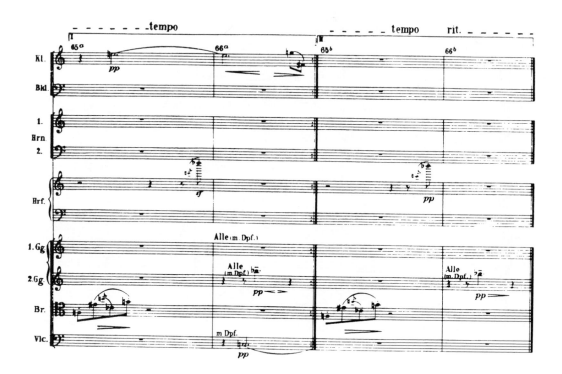

The Symphony Op. 21 (1928) is for nine solo instruments. It is in two movements, the first in sonata form and the second a theme with seven variations. Some idea of Webern's use of the serial technique may be obtained from the markings on a reduced score of the first 13 measures:

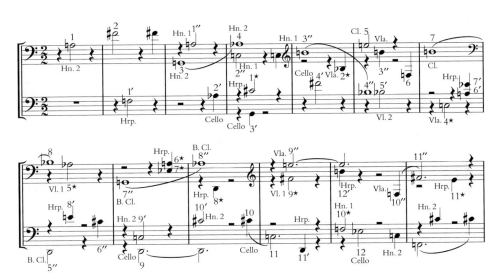

What may be called the "original" form of the tone row is designated by the numbers 1, 2, etc. (some analysts start the numbering with 0; note that the second half of the row is the retrograde of the first half and that consequently the retrograde form of the entire row is a duplicate of its original form); the numbers 1', 2', etc., designate an inversion (or a retrograde inversion) of the original form, beginning a major third lower; 1″, 2″, etc., designate an inversion (or retrograde inversion) beginning at the original pitch. The C♯ in measure 4 begins a statement of the original form of the row (or its retrograde) transposed a major third upward. To be noted also in this example is the characteristically spare, open texture, and the numerous rests in all the parts. Thus every single note counts, and the ensemble becomes a succession of tiny points or wisps of sound; hence the term "pointillism" to describe this technique.

What meets the ear is a static mosaic of instrumental colors. But close study reveals many constructive strategies. For example, at the outset the two horns are in canon by contrary motion; then the same canonic voices are continued in the clarinet and bass clarinet. Meanwhile the harp begins another canon by contrary motion, using the same intervallic sequences (disregarding octave register) as the first canon but with a new scheme of durations and rests. A complete analysis would show that the piece is very tightly organized, that entire sections are mirror images of other sections, and that the movement consists of an exposition, development, and recapitulation.

142 OLIVIER MESSIAEN (1908–1992)

Quatuor pour la fin du temps

Liturgie de cristal (first movement)

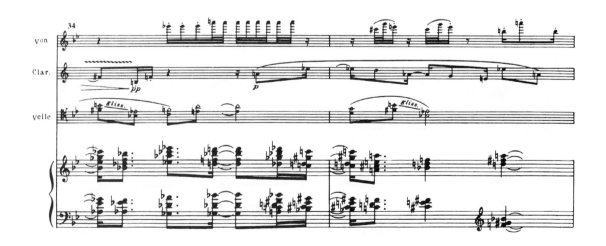

Messiaen composed the *Quartet for the End of Time* in 1940–41 for violin, cello, clarinet, and piano, to be performed with three fellow prisoners in a German camp. It consists of the following movements: *Liturgie de cristal* (Crystal Liturgy); *Vocalise, pour l'ange qui annonce la fin du temps* (Vocalise for the Angel Who Announces the End of Time); *Abîme des oiseaux* (Abyss of the Birds); *Intermède* (Intermezzo); *Louange à l'éternité de Jésus* (Praise to the Eternity of Jesus); *Danse de la fureur, pour les sept trompettes* (Dance of the Fury for the Seven Trumpets); *Fouillis d'arcs-en-ciel, pour l'ange qui annonce la fin du temps'* (Medley of Rainbows for the Angel Who Announces the End of Time); and *Louange à l'immortalité de Jésus* (Praise to the Immortality of Jesus). The angel is that of the Apocalypse "who lifts his hand towards heaven, proclaiming 'Time will be no more'."

The quartet is a study of time: measured, finite time, and timelessness or eternity. Although the quartet lacks a text, it is a piece of sacred music, as is a great deal of this composer's output. Religion is not so much on the surface as the motivation and goal for creative effort. Nature is also ever present in his compositions, often in the form of birdsong, as in the opening dialogue between the blackbird (clarinet) and a nightingale (flute) in the first movement. The rhythm is also that of nature, having a pulse but no regular meter.

Messiaen compared the movement *Crystal Liturgy,* to "the harmonious silence of the firmament." The clarinet is in the foreground, while the cello's harmonics paint an ethereal background and the bird sounds in the flute lend distance and depth to the scene. The movement illustrates several aspects of Messiaen's creative method. A serious student of both Western music history and the music of India, he was evidently inspired by fourteenth-century isorhythm as well as by Indian music to base this movement on the repetitions of extended rhythmic patterns. This "rhythmic pedal," as Messiaen called it, though based on the rhythmic pattern of the Hindu *râgavardhana,* resembles a medieval *talea*. It is complemented by an overlapping pitch-pattern analogous to the medieval *color*. The two together constitute a melodic-harmonic ostinato. The isorhythmic pattern as notated in the piano part is shown in Example a, its resolution into integral note values in b.

The notation varies according to where the pattern falls in the metric scheme. When the pattern is resolved into untied note values, as in Example b, it becomes evident that its measures are of unequal length. The additional three sixteenths in the first measure and one sixteenth in the last, Messiaen called "valeurs ajoutées," or added note values. Messiaen also used what he called a "non-retrogradable rhythm," a pattern whose second half is a retrograde of the first half, so that the retrograde of the whole pattern is identical to the original form, which is therefore not retrogradable. Such a unit exists in a self-contained frame of time and aspires toward the composer's goal of achieving a timelessness in his music. An instance occurs in the cello (measures 2–10; see Example c, the notation in the cello part, and d, its resolution into integral note values).

a. Rhythmic pattern in the piano

Bien modéré, en poudroiement harmonieux

Piano

pp legato (très enveloppé de pédale)

b. Resolution in integral values

c. Rhythmic pattern in the cello

d. Resolution in integral values

center

143 CHARLES IVES (1874–1954)

They Are There!

A War Song March

then the world will shout the bat-tle cry of Free - dom.

hear the whole un - i-verse shout-ing, the bat-tle cry of Free - dom.

There's a time in many a life
when it's do though facing death
and our soldier boys will do their part
that people can live,
in a world where all will have a say.
They're conscious always of their country's aim,
which is liberty for all.
Hip hip Hooray you'll hear them say,
as they go to the fighting front.
Brave boys are now in action,
they are there, they will help to free the world.
They are fighting for the right,
but when it comes to might
they are there, they are there, they are there.
As the Allies beat up all the warhogs,
the boys'll be there fighting hard, and
then the world will shout the battle cry of Freedom.

When we're through this cursed war,
all started by a sneaking gouger,
making slaves of men,
then let all the people rise,
and stand together in brave, kind humanity.
Most wars are made by small stupid selfish bossing
    groups,
while the people have no say.
But there'll come a day Hip hip Hooray,
when they'll smash all dictators to the wall.
Then it's build a people's world nation,
Hooray.
Eve'ry honest country's free to live its own native
    life.
They will stand for the right,
but if it comes to might
they are there, they are there, they are there.
Then the people, not just politicians,
will rule their own lands and lives.
Then you'll hear the whole universe shouting
the battle cry of Freedom.

Tenting in a new camp ground,
Tenting tonight,
Tenting in a new camp ground.
For it's rally 'round the Flag of the
people's new free world,
shouting the battle cry of Freedom.

Ives wrote this song in 1917, the year that the United States joined the Allies of World War I—Russia, France, Britain, Serbia, Italy, Montenegro, Belgium, and Japan—in fighting the Central Powers: Germany, Austria-Hungary, and the Ottoman Empire. To adapt the song for performance during World War II, the composer made some minor changes in the text and entitled it "They Are There!" resulting in the version published in 1961 and reprinted here. The medium is a unison chorus and a standard symphony orchestra, with the violins split into four instead of two parts, and the addition of piano and tubular chimes.

The text is mostly in the rhythm of prose. Rhymed lines paraphrased from patriotic songs occasionally ring out, sometimes with the pertinent tune but mostly not. An example is "Tenting in a new camp ground" (misquoting "Tenting on the old camp ground," paired with new music) at measure 34. Similarly the tunes of patriotic songs leap out of a melodic continuity that has its own logic apart from them. The quotations and misquotations seem less like semi-conscious borrowings than deliberate invocations of familiar songs for their power to add punch to the message, like vivid images or rhetorical figures in poetry. The most obvious of the musical allusions are the opening fragment of *O Columbia, the gem of the ocean* (also known as *The Red, White, and Blue*) in the unison chorus at measures 19–20; the incipit of *Dixie's Land* immediately following in the higher woodwinds; at measure 23, the unison chorus misquoting the *Battle Hymn of the Republic*; and, just before the end (measure 49), a bit of the *Star-Spangled Banner* in the brass, followed by *Reveille* in the trumpets and flutes.

The diatonic and martial lines of the unison chorus are accompanied by harmonically appropriate bass notes and animated harmony in the lower strings and brass, while the upper strings and the winds either oppose different diatonic material (such as *Dixie's Land*) or indulge in chromatic passage work and chromatic quasi-ostinatos. This passage work is sometimes deliberately cacophonous, as when the strings play fast interlocking major sevenths (measure 27, first heard as chords in measure 18), or quadruple parallel seconds (measure 52). The effect, especially in the final pages, is that of a carnival in which one hears alternately snatches of an anthem played by a brass band or a military call by a fife and bugle corps, while a noisy crowd is milling about.

RUTH CRAWFORD SEEGER (1901–1953)

Violin Sonata

Buoyant (second movement)*

*Accidentals apply only to the notes directly following.

Ruth Crawford wrote her Violin Sonata in 1926. It consists of four movements: Vivace, agitato; Buoyant; Mistico, intenso; and Allegro.

The second movement is built on a nine-beat syncopated ostinato in the piano's left hand divided by an accent into $\frac{5}{8}$ plus $\frac{4}{8}$. After zigzag leaps of major seventh, minor seventh, major sixth, and augmented fourth, the ostinato winds up with a whole-tone run and a leap of a minor ninth to start the next recurrence. During the first seven statements, while the right hand is silent, the violin floats above the left hand's spiky waves with a staccato diatonic idea that ends with a whole-tone tail (the last six pitches of measure 6 contain all the steps of a whole-tone scale).

The ostinato is tonally stable until measure 10, when it begins to modulate. After an interruption of three measures and a cadenza by the violin (measure 19), it migrates to a higher register, where it remains stable again (the intervals varying slightly). Another modulatory section that alternates simultaneities of the only two possible whole-tone scales (mm. 38–39) leads to a passage in $\frac{10}{8}$, in which the bass and violin join in a craggy organum of parallel tritones (mm. 44–50) while the piano's right hand takes up the violin's staccato theme.

Aaron Copland (1900–1990)

Appalachian Spring

Variations on *'Tis the Gift to be Simple* (excerpt)

a) Original Shaker melody and text

'Tis the gift to be sim-ple, 'tis the gift to be free, 'Tis the gift to come down where we ought to be, And when we find our-selves in the place just right, 'Twill be in the val-ley of love and de-light. When true sim-pli-ci-ty is gain'd, To bow and to bend we shan't be a-sham'd, To turn, turn will be our de-light 'Till by turn-ing, turn-ing we come round right.

Reprinted by permission from Edward D. Andrews, *The Gift to be Simple* (New York: Dover, 1940), p. 136.

b) *Appalachian Spring* (excerpt)

Copland incorporated in this music for ballet variations on an actual folk tune, the Shaker hymn *'Tis the Gift to be Simple* (a), which is subtly transfigured and its essence absorbed in a work that sincerely expresses the pastoral spirit in authentically American terms.

The sparse accompaniment to the tune in the statement and first variation, with its wide spacing of chords, empty octaves, and fifths, suggests country fiddling. These harmonies and the carefully calculated instrumental colors are characteristic of this composer. Copland sometimes used any or all notes of the diatonic scale for vertical combinations, as illustrated in the harmonization of the tune from Rehearsal 64. A characteristic sonority produced by this means is the opening chord of *Appalachian Spring,* which, with its derivatives and amplifications, serves as a unifying device, returning from time to time throughout the work (see example below).

146 WILLIAM GRANT STILL (1895–1978)

Afro-American Symphony

Animato (third movement)

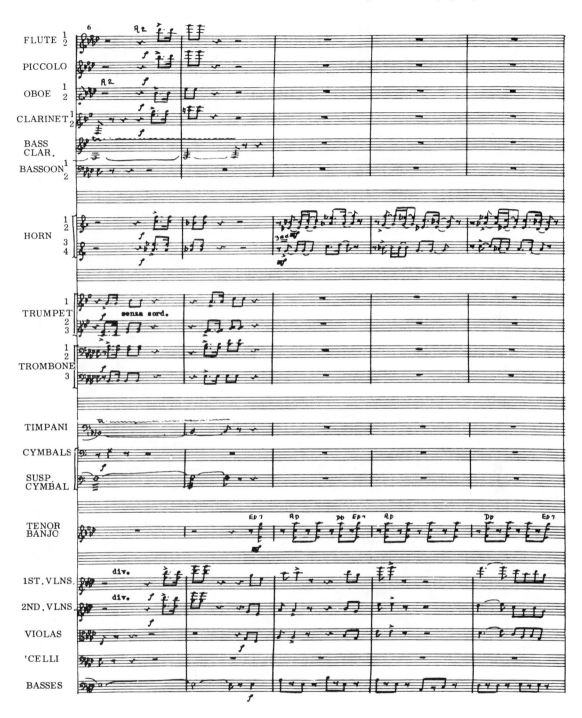

46
FLUTE 1 2 3
mp graziosoamente
p
OBOE 1 2
mp graziosamente
CLARINET 1 2
mp graziosamente
p
BASS CLAR.
mp
BASSOON 1 2
mp graziosamente
HORN 2 3 4
mp mf
TROMBONE 1 2 3
TUBA
HARP
1ST. VLNS.
2ND. VLNS.
VIOLAS
'CELLI
BASSES
pizz.
f marcato

(*)Please do not retard the 2nd. and 3rd measures of this page.

(*) At upper ends of the strings.

Still wrote this symphony, his first of five, in 1930 and revised it in 1969 to produce the version presented here. Originally Still gave each movement a subtitle: 1. *Longings*; 2. *Sorrows*; 3. *Humor*; 4. *Aspirations.* He also linked each movement to some verses from a poem by Paul Laurence Dunbar.

The third movement is a colorful, cleverly orchestrated scherzo, its syncopations suggesting a dance. The lowered third and seventh "blue notes" are prominent melodically and harmonically, particularly in the transformations of the opening motive (see example a below), which evolves into a sixteen-bar tune (example b). An accompaniment of off-beat banjo chords punctuates the orchestral texture. The eight measures that make up the first half of this tune neatly fit the verses of Dunbar that pertain to this movement:

> An' we'll shout ouah halleluyahs,
> On dat mighty reck'nin day.

This melody returns toward the end, transformed in the first violins playing octaves divisi (measure 77), the blue notes standing out even more than before. Coinciding with the second half of the melody (measure 83), the main theme from the first movement is developed in the trumpet and trombones as a counterpoint to the violins, the banjo chords accompanying both.

a. Opening motive

b. Evolved tune

ELLIOTT CARTER (b. 1908)
String Quartet No. 2

Introduction and Allegro fantastico

Introduction

attacca

I

Allegro fantastico (♩ = 112)

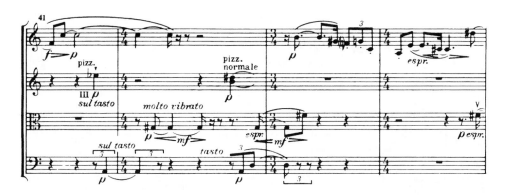

★ ⌐⌐ = important secondary part
       wichtige Nebenstimme

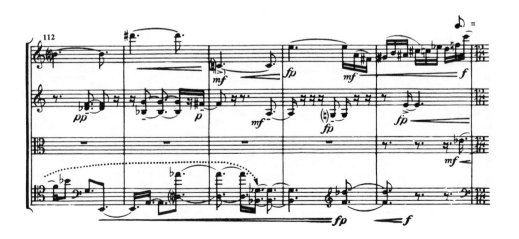

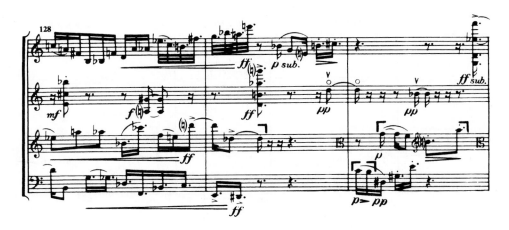

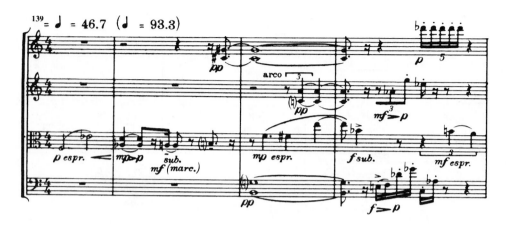

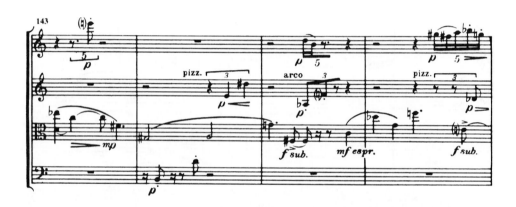

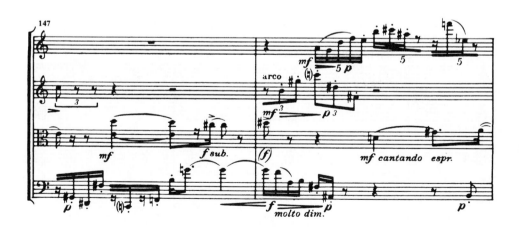

One of Elliott Carter's important contributions has been to develop a new
approach to changes in tempo and rhythm among instrumental parts and
among sections of a continuous movement. Early in his career, he devised a
technique that came to be called "metrical modulation" but which he later
preferred to think of as "tempo modulation." By means of proportional
changes, similar to those of the fifteenth century, individual parts may speed
up or slow down in proportional increments with respect to other parts, or

an entire ensemble may thus accelerate or decelerate. In the First String Quartet, Carter imparted a sharp profile to individual parts by having one player change speed while others continued at the previous tempo.

The Second Quartet individualizes the parts not only with respect to tempo and rhythm but also general character. In a prefatory note to the score and parts, the composer asked that players observe tempos and note values strictly and that each player "maintain a slightly different character of playing from the others." The first violin should display the greatest variety of character, sometimes precise, at other times free, fantastic, and virtuosic. The second violin's part has conventional rhythms that must be observed strictly in an orderly but sometimes humorous manner, and it alternates between arco and pizzicato. The viola plays expressively and elastically, indulging in rubato and glissandos. The cello often has continuous accelerando approximated by written note values and indicated by a dotted arrow line (for example, measures 1–2, 5–6), or it may have a similarly notated ritardando, but mostly it plays in strict time. In this way each part takes on a personality and pattern of behavior that distinguishes it and interacts with others in the ensemble as if in a quartet from an opera. In the Second Quartet each of the instruments has a chance to exhibit its idiosyncrasies in an extended solo or cadenza, as the first violin's long solo and the viola's extended cadenza in the first movement. In thus personalizing the instruments, Carter may have been influenced by Charles Ives's Second Quartet, whose three movements Ives described as 1. *Four Men Have Discussions, Conversations;* 2. *Arguments and Fights;* and 3. *Contemplation.**

Independence and individualism also characterize the way the parts develop their melodic and rhythmic material. In the Introduction, the first violin dwells on minor thirds and perfect fifths (including double stops), with some melodic semitones, and breaks out with spurts of sixteenth and thirty-second notes. The second violin develops the sound of the major third melodically and in double stops mainly in longer durations. The viola in a similar way specializes in tritones, through expressionistic gestures, glissandos, rapid crescendos and diminuendos, and sudden off-beat exclamations. The cello emphasizes perfect fourths, as in the opening measures, where the fourth is heard first melodically, then in double stops, and later mixes these with minor sixths. The behavioral patterns become compulsive in the Allegro fantastico, all the parts fantasizing in their own fashion, most prominently the first violin. The first movement ends with a cadenza for the viola, the other parts sometimes accompanying, sometimes commenting sympathetically or mockingly on its lyrical outpourings.

Carter designated the main divisions of the quartet—to be played without interruption—as Introduction, 1. Allegro fantastico; 2. Presto scherzando; 3. Andante espressivo; and 4. Allegro. In movement 3, the parts for the first time imitate each other's contours, each in its own way. In the final Allegro a kind of reconciliation occurs, and the parts become more coordinated and homogeneous.

*Charles Ives, *Memos,* ed. John Kirkpatrick (New York: Norton, 1972), p. 75.

148 GEORGE CRUMB (b. 1929)

Black Angels, Thirteen Images from the Dark Land,
for Electric String Quartet

Images 4 to 9

a) Image 4: *Devil-Music*

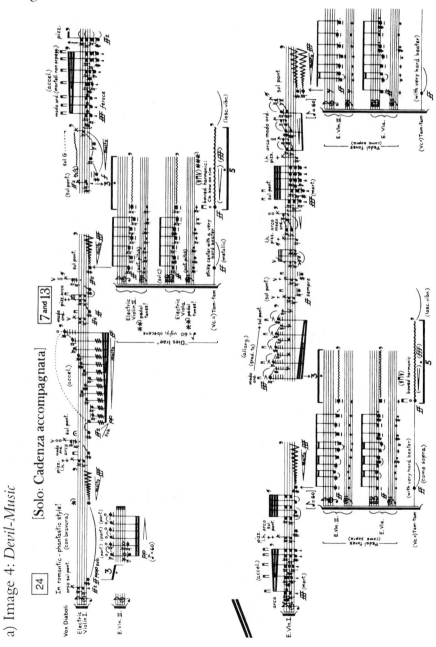

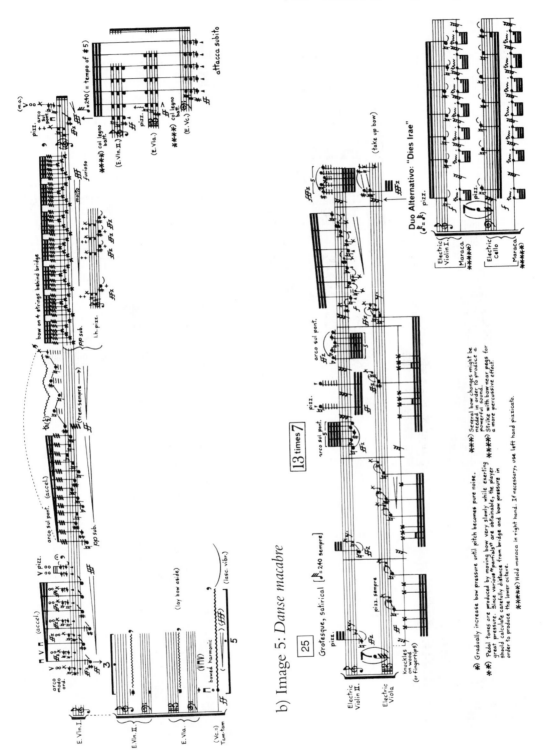

b) Image 5: *Danse macabre*

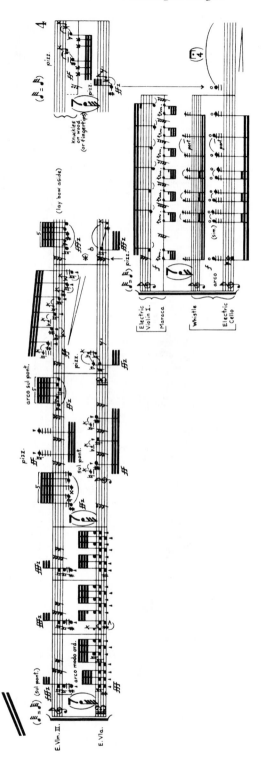

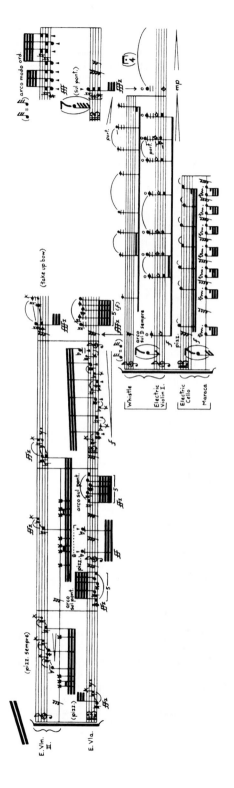

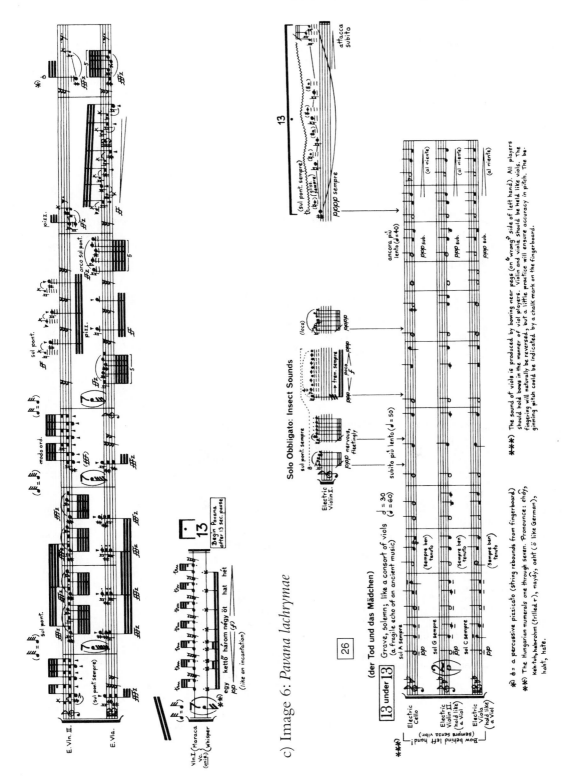

c) Image 6: *Pavana lachrymae*

d) Image 7: *Threnody II: Black Angels!*

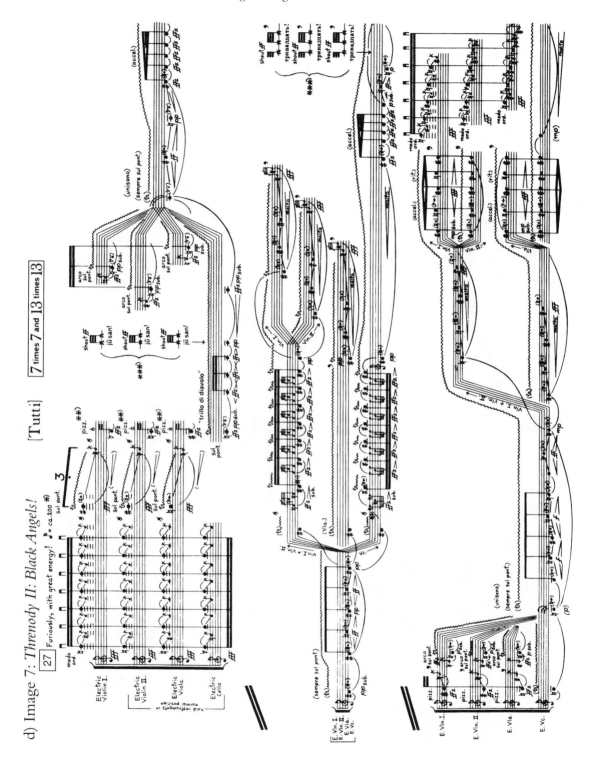

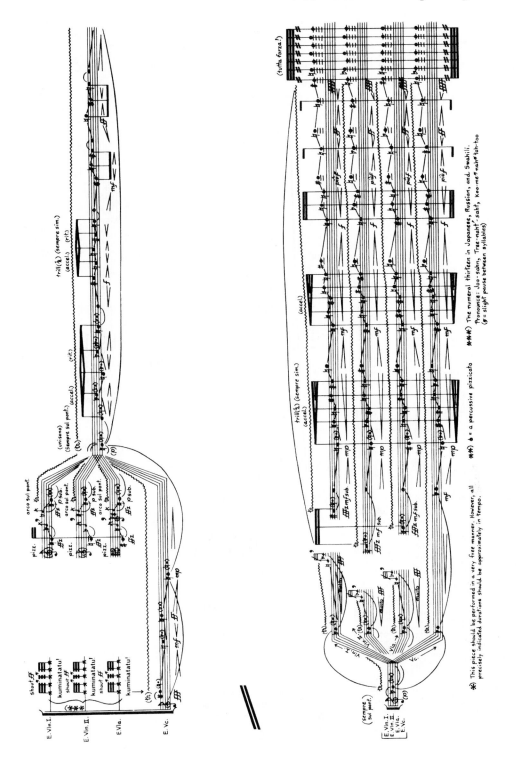

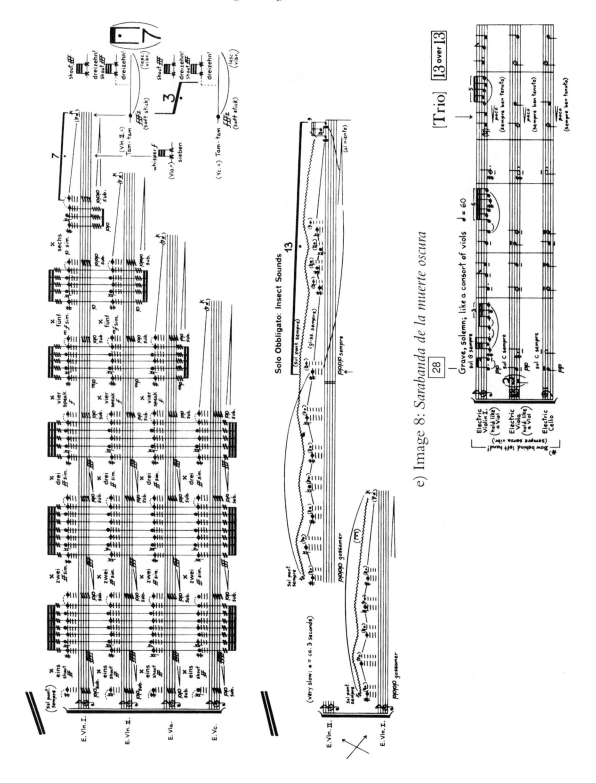

e) Image 8: *Sarabanda de la muerte oscura*

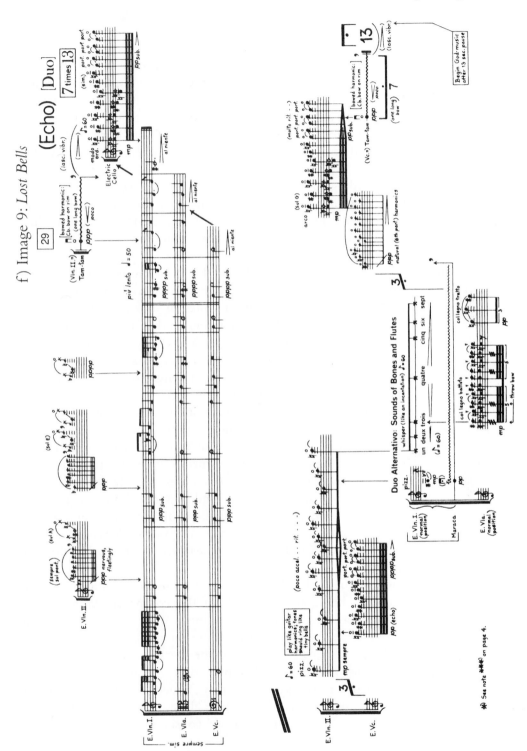

The *Thirteen Images from the Dark Land* express Crumb's darker thoughts, fears, and feelings in the troubled world of the late 1960s. He inscribed at the end of the score: "finished on Friday the Thirteenth, March 1970 (in tempore belli)." *In tempore belli* (in time of war) refers to the Vietnam War, the American involvement in which many artists and intellectuals deplored. Life and death, good and evil, god and devil are evoked through a veil of mysterious sound.

The work, according to the composer, represents three stages in a journey of the soul: fall from grace (the section marked "Departure," including Images 1 to 5), spiritual annihilation (the section marked "Absence," including Images 6 to 9), and redemption (the section marked "Return," including Images 10 to 13).

The string quartet is electronically amplified to produce a surrealistic effect of dreamlike juxtapositions. The composer also explored unusual means of bowing, such as to produce pedal tones, or striking the strings near the pegs with the bow, holding the bow underhand in the manner of viol players, bowing between the left-hand finger and the pegs, as well as more conventional glissandos, *sul ponticello,* and percussive pizzicato. These effects are not mere striving for novelty; the composer sought to create with them a nightmarish atmosphere as a substrate for his poetic message.

Like a number of his contemporaries, Crumb liked to quote older music. Image 4, *Devil-Music,* and 5, *Danse macabre,* quote the *Dies irae* melody. *Pavana lachrymae,* the title of Image 6, leads us to expect Dowland's Pavane on his air *Flow, my tears* (NAWM 45), but it turns out to be a foil for a citation from Schubert's *Death and the Maiden* quartet made to sound like antique viol-consort music through underhand bowing. Similar conceits are crucial in the *Danse macabre:* the tritone is the central motive, representing the supposedly medieval derogation of this interval as *diabolus in musica* (devil in music), and a quotation of Tartini's *Devil's Trill.* The eighth image is an ancient Sarabanda.

The grouping of notes, chords, and figures into units of 7 and 13 is symbolic, these numbers being in the words of the composer "fateful numbers"—that is, numbers that are considered lucky or unlucky. At the same time, counting semitones downward, 7 mediates the interval 13 in the chord $D\sharp$-A-E (13-7-1), prominent in several of the Images, particularly No. 7, *Threnody II: Black Angels!* (the cycle begins with *Threnody I*), a lamentation that mediates the work in the same way that A mediates the chord. These remarks do not begin to exhaust the fleeting allusions, symbols, and obsessions that pass through the listener's confused consciousness as in a dream.

MILTON BABBITT (b. 1916)

Philomel, for Soprano, Recorded Soprano, and Synthesized Sound

Section I

Commissioned by the Ford Foundation for Bethany Beardslee. This "score" is a complete vocal part, and—with exceptions—a total representation of the rhythmic and pitch content of the synthesized and recorded accompaniment in all those sections of the work in which the singer participates. The exceptions occur when, to avoid notational complexity, the rhythmic representation is only closely approximate, and registral relations are simplified. The tape interludes, in which the singer does not participate, are neither notated nor cued. Accidentals affect only those notes which they immediately precede, with the exception of tied notes.

INTERLUDE (Tape)

Not true tears — Not true trees —

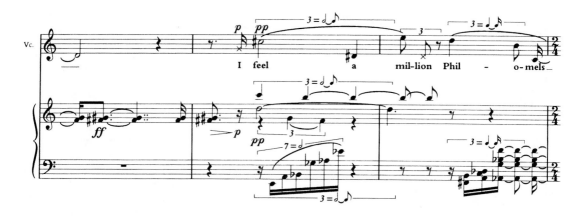

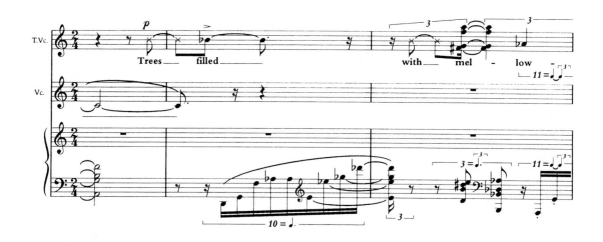

INTERLUDE

INTERLUDE

TAPE VOICE: Pillowing melody, honey unheard —

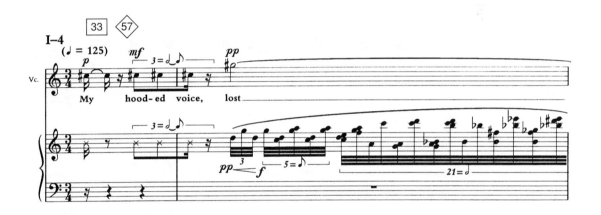

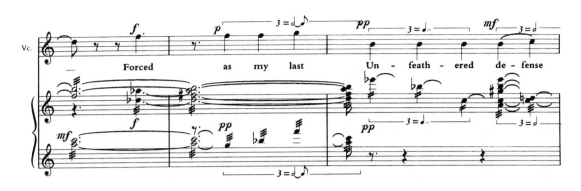

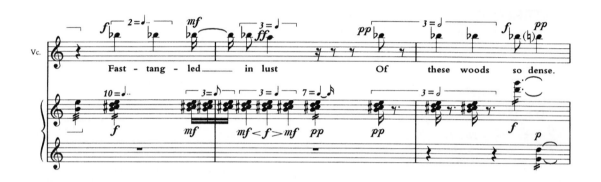

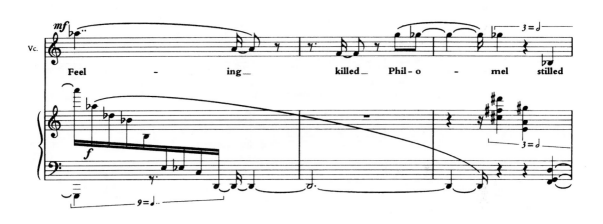

INTERLUDE

TAPE VOICE: Feeling killed, Philomel stilled, Her honey unfulfilled.

TAPE

(Recorded Soprano)
(Eeeeeeeeeeeeeeeeee)

PHILOMEL

Eeeeeeeeeeeeeeeeeee! `
Eeeeeeeeeeeeeeeeeee!
Eeeeeeeeeeeeeeeeeee!
I feel
Feel a million trees
And the heat of trees

TAPE

Not true trees—

PHILOMEL

Feel a million tears

TAPE

Not true tears—
Not true trees—

PHILOMEL

Is it Tereus I feel?

TAPE

Not Tereus: not a true Tereus—

PHILOMEL

Feel a million filaments;
Fear the tearing, the feeling
Trees, of ephemeral leaves

Trees tear,
And I bear
Families of tears
I feel a million Philomels

TAPE

Trees filled with mellowing
Felonous fame—

PHILOMEL

I feel trees in my hair
And on the ground,
Honeymelons fouling
My knees and feet
Soundlessly in my
Flight through the forest;
I founder in quiet.

Here I find only
Miles of felted silence
Unwinding behind me,
Lost, lost in the wooded night.

TAPE

Pillowing melody,
Honey unheard—

PHILOMEL

My hooded voice, lost
Lost, as my first
Unhoneyed tongue;
Forced, as my last
Unfeathered defense
Fast-tangled in lust

Of these woods so dense.
Emptied, unfeeling and unfilled
By trees here where no birds have
    trilled—
Feeling killed
Philomel stilled
Her honey unfulfilled.

TAPE

Feeling killed
Philomel stilled
Her honey unfulfilled

PHILOMEL

What is that sound?
A voice found?
Broken, the bound
Of silence, beyond
Violence of human sound,
As if a new self
Could be founded on sound.
The trees are astounded!
What is this humming?
I am becoming
My own song . . .

—JOHN HOLLANDER

Philomel (1964) combines synthesized sounds, prerecorded tape, and live performance. The soprano soloist is heard against a tape that incorporates an altered recording, a kind of distorted echo, of her own voice, together with electronic sounds. The poem, written expressly for this setting by John Hollander, is based on the fable in Ovid (*Metamorphoses* 6:412–674). Procne, wife of Tereus, king of Thrace, is eager to see her sister Philomela after many years and sends Tereus to fetch her. On the return trip Tereus rapes Philomela in a Thracian wood and cuts out her tongue to prevent disclosure, but his guilt is exposed nevertheless by a tapestry in which Philomela weaves her story. Procne, horrified, avenges herself against her husband by killing their son and feeding Tereus from the butchered corpse. Angry, Tereus pursues the two sisters, but before he can catch them the gods transform him into a hoopoe bird, Procne into a swallow, and Philomela into a nightingale. In the metamorphosis Philomela regains her voice. The sung text begins at this point.

John Hollander's poem (and Babbitt's composition) is in three sections. In the first Philomel screams as she recalls the pain of violation; dazed, she expresses her feelings in vivid but incoherent images. She runs through the forest in fear and confusion. In Section 2, Philomel seeks answers about her predicament from a thrush, a hawk, an owl, and a gull. In the third section, she sings a strophic lament, joined in refrains by her taped voice.

An unusual feature for electronic music, here is a score representing the voice part, the prerecorded voice, and the accompanying synthesized sounds. The tape voice often answers by distorting the soloist's line or, speaking, comments like a Greek chorus. The score gives evidence that every detail in the vocal sections was worked out in serial terms. The vocal sections alternate with unnotated synthesized and tape interludes that are more freely composed and are not represented in the score.

The vocal melody is extremely disjunct, with leaps of major sevenths, ninths, and even elevenths. Some of the notes are sung in Sprechstimme, marked by an X instead of a notehead, and expressive glissandos punctuate some phrases. The pitch-class E, the first note sung by the tape voice, is central to the construction of the opening passage. The twelve-tone row is stated, then transposed, in such a way that E becomes successively the first, second, third, fourth, and fifth pitch-class in the row. With each unfolding of the row, the tape voice claims more of the row's pitch-classes up to E—in the second measure two, in the third three, and so on. The accompaniment each time claims the remainder of the row or aggregate (the twelve pitch-classes of the chromatic scale). The first sonority, as the taped soprano screams "Eeeeeee" on E, contains all twelve pitch-classes, covering the entire spectrum from D' to e'. Subsequent simultaneities are less populated, with increasingly arpeggiated and pointillistic unfoldings of the row. The top e' is heard as a steady pedal note through the first eight measures. When Philomel's natural voice enters, it begins on F, and E is now the last member of the row, appearing as the highest note in the accompaniment in measure 9.

Like Schoenberg in *Pierrot lunaire*, Babbitt tore some leaves from the book of the sixteenth-century madrigalists. The pitch E for the scream is a madrigalian conceit, as are the synthesized trills on the word "trilled." He went beyond the madrigalists in the second section of the poem, where, instead of bird imitations, he introduced recorded birdsong.

Gunther Schuller (b. 1925)

Seven Studies on Themes of Paul Klee

Nos. 3 and 5

a) No. 3. *Kleiner blauer Teufel*

*) Opt. - Legato - Tongued
ad lib.: gebunden oder gestoßen

Sept. 13, 1959

b) No. 5. *Arabische Stadt*

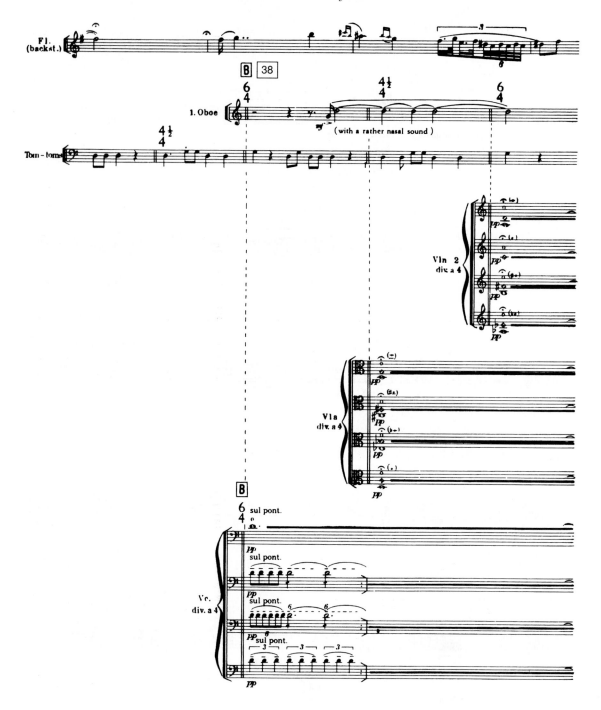

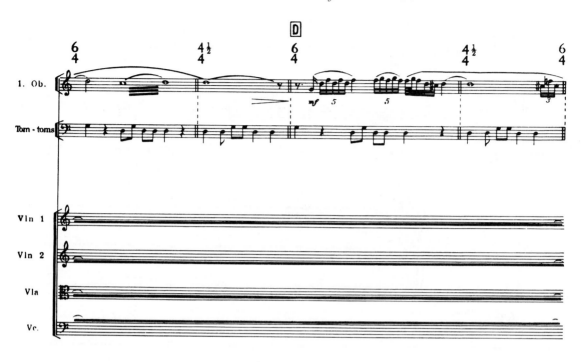

* Timp., muffle with cloth or rubber pad ;
high c can also be played on Tom · tom

Timp., dämpfen mit Stoff oder Gummi · Platte ;
c' kann auch auf Tom · tom gespielt werden.

September 21st, 1959

The *Seven Studies* were Schuller's response to a commission from the Ford Foundation and the Minneapolis Symphony Orchestra in 1959 which stipulated that the work would be played by nine other symphony orchestras. A survey in 1964–65 showed that it turned out to have been the most frequently played orchestral work by an American composer since 1938. The two movements selected illustrate the influence of vernacular and non-Western music on the work of a sensitive American composer.

a) The composer remarked that "the comic-seriousness of Klee's famous cubist demon," *Kleiner blauer Teufel* (Little Blue Devil) of 1933, "evolved into a jazz ('Third Stream') piece with a perky fragmented tune and 'blue' instrumental colorings." Several jazz elements spark Schuller's musical portrayal of Klee's blue devil in the "Third Stream" idiom that he pioneered. A slapped double bass playing four to the bar, countered by syncopated beats on snare drum and suspended cymbals struck by wooden sticks or brush, maintains a steady rhythmic frame for a blues pattern. Muted horns and trumpets constitute the brass section. Riffs on the vibraphone and low clarinets enhance the jazz coloring.

Schuller reduced the conventional twelve-bar blues harmonic progression to nine measures. The pattern announced in the solo double bass at measures 15–23 is repeated in measures 24–32, 34–42, 44–54 (extended by lazy triplets in the sixth measure), 55–63, and 65–73. Against this harmonic background, if we assume B as the tonality, the lowered third and fifth of blues are prominent in the angular theme suggested by Klee's geometrized figure (trumpet, measures 24–32). Each of the subsequent choruses that make variations on the nine-bar pattern features different instruments: flutes, clarinets, and trumpets (third chorus, measures 34–42), vibraphone and strings (fourth chorus), pizzicato strings (fifth chorus), and flutes, clarinets, and trumpets (sixth chorus).

b) Schuller remarked that *Arabische Stadt* (Arab Village), Klee's painting of 1922, "is an abstracted aerial view of a town baking in the bright North African desert sun. A beholder of such a scene—floating, as it were, above the village—might hear the often simultaneous chant of Arab melodies: the melancholy distant flute, blending with throbbing drums and the nasal dance tunes of the oboe." In preparing for the piece he consulted sources on Arab music, and either quoted or adapted authentic Middle Eastern melodies.

The opening flute melody played backstage in a free, meterless rhythm simulates improvisation on a *maqām* or Arabic mode in which the middle interval of a tetrachord is wider than two semitones (for example, B–C–D#–E). Grace notes, turns, trills, and ornamenting arabesques characterize the melody. When an oboe enters at Rehearsal B, three independent performers are represented—the distant flutist, a tom-tom player, and the oboist—each entertaining its own circle, producing random clashes similar to those of Charles Ives's famous competing marching bands. The oboe, moreover, "improvises" on a different *maqām* —G′–B♭′–C′–C#′–D–F. Its melody consists largely of tremolos and turns around the notes *D* and *F*.

In the Allegro, the instruments are asked to simulate a *maqām* in which the lowest interval of the tetrachord B½♭–C–D–E½♭ is three quarter-tones (a semitone and a half) and the top one is also three quarter-tones. The oboe uses special fingerings to produce pitches that are a quarter tone lower than written, and the harp tunes the *B* and *E* strings a quarter tone flat. The solo viola similarly fingers these notes flat. Since the players estimate the size of the quarter tone slightly differently, they are minutely out of tune, causing a haunting dissonance characteristic of Middle Eastern ensembles. The cello provides a nasal drone by bowing heavily. This Allegro section, suggesting music for a belly dance, is partly in a steady meter and partly in shifting additive meters combining duple and triple units.

Schuller evidently took care to make the human actors missing in Klee's village scene authentic native musicians; he was not content to conjure up some exotic sounds for atmosphere's sake.

STEVE REICH (b. 1936)

151

Violin Phase

In the version for a single violinist and three-track tape, the performer first records bar 1 over and over again for one to five minutes. Then, after rewinding the tape, the violinist super-imposes repetitions of the same pattern of notes, but now four eighth notes ahead of the first track, as at bar 7. The performer then rewinds the tape again and records the pattern four eighth notes ahead of track 2, as at bar 18. The best three to seven repetitions are made into a tape loop, resulting in the ostinato shown in bar 18, fourth staff from the top. The violinist performs the composition against this ostinato by playing at first in unison with the first track, then accelerating until he or she is one eighth note ahead of track 1, when the tempo is held for a number of repeats, after which the process of alternate acceleration and synchronization with the tape continues.

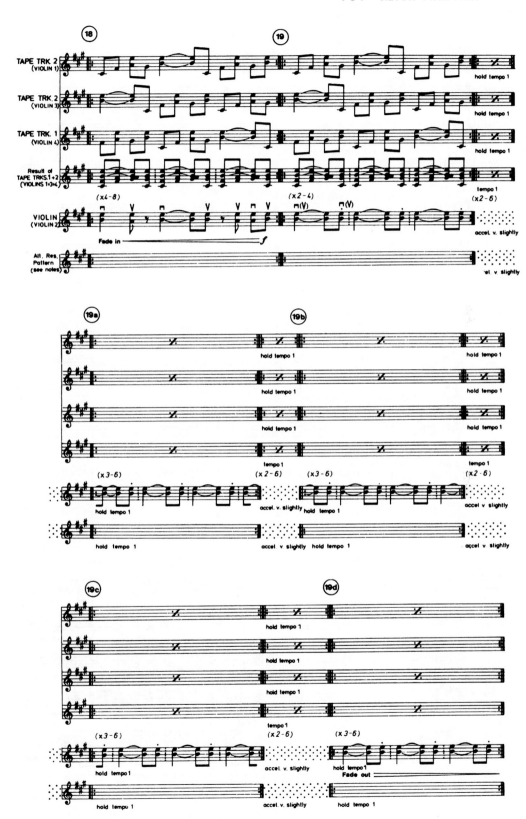

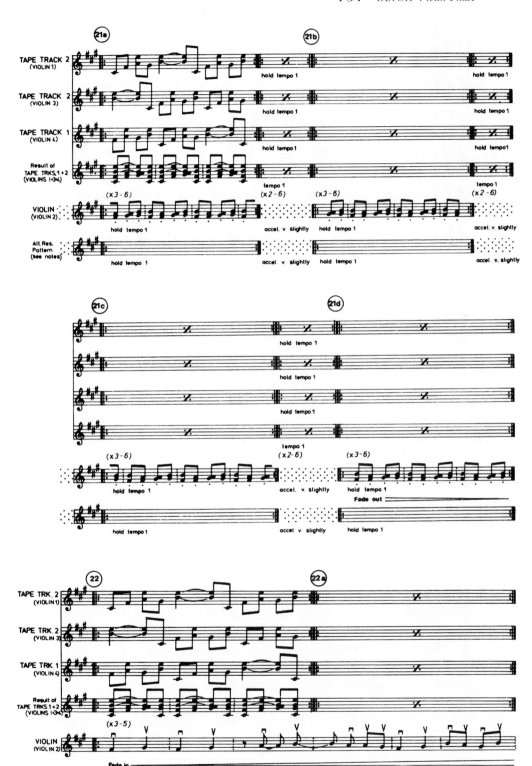

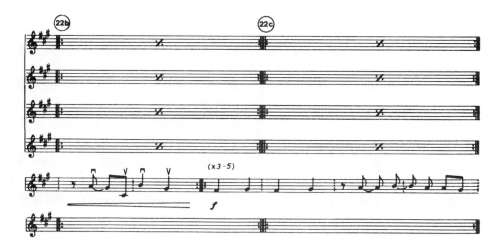

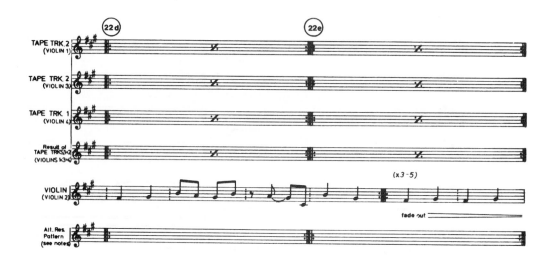

Reich, who represents the minimalist movement in this anthology, developed a quasi-canonic procedure in which musicians play the same material slightly out of phase with each other. He was led to this strategy by superimposing tapes of the same speaking voice in such a way that one tape, moving slightly faster, got out of step with the other. He applied the idea to two pianos in *Piano Phase* (1967), and in *Violin Phase* (1967) he juxtaposed a live violinist with a second one on tape. The piece evolved into a published version (1979) for four violinists or for a single violinist with three synchronous recording tracks.

In the version for a single violinist and three-track tape, the performer first records measure 1 over and over again for one to five minutes. Then, after rewinding the tape, the violinist superimposes repetitions of the same pattern of notes, but now four eighth notes ahead of the first track, as at measure 7. The performer then rewinds the tape again and records the pattern four eighth notes ahead of track 2, as in measure 18. The best three to seven repetitions are made into a tape loop, resulting in the ostinato shown in the fourth staff at measure 18.

The violinist performs the composition against this ostinato by playing at first in unison with the first track, then accelerating until the violinist is one eighth note ahead of track 1, when the tempo is held for a number of repeats, after which the process of alternate acceleration and synchronization with the tape continues. The piece also employs fade-ins and fade-outs by both the live performer and individual tape tracks.

152 GEORGE ROCHBERG (b. 1918)

Nach Bach, Fantasy for Harpsichord or Piano

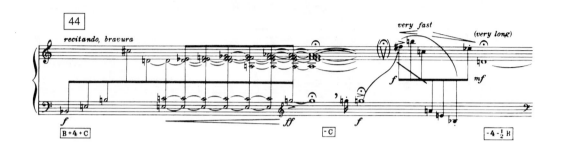

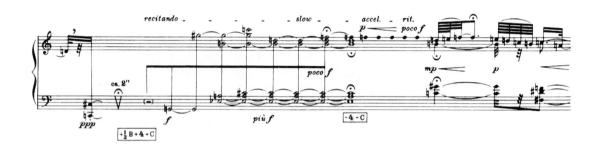

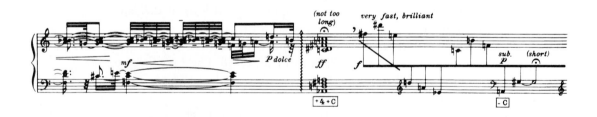

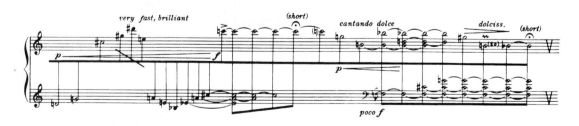

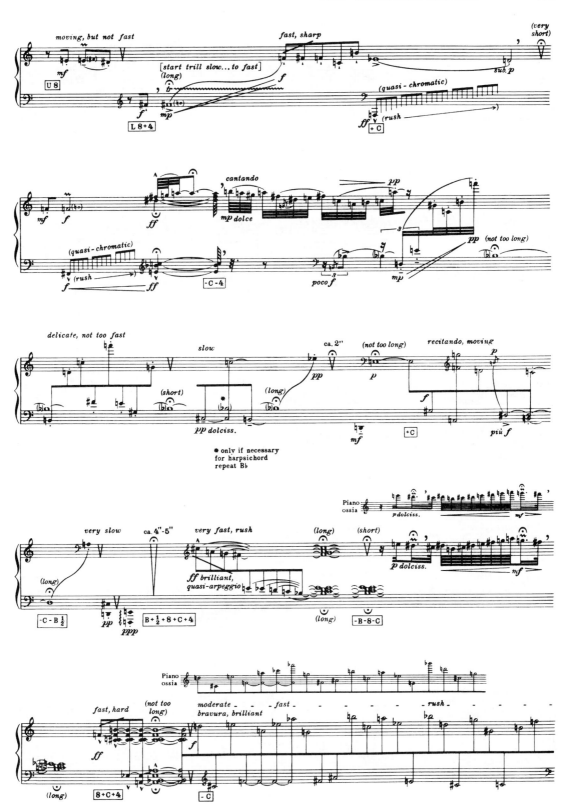

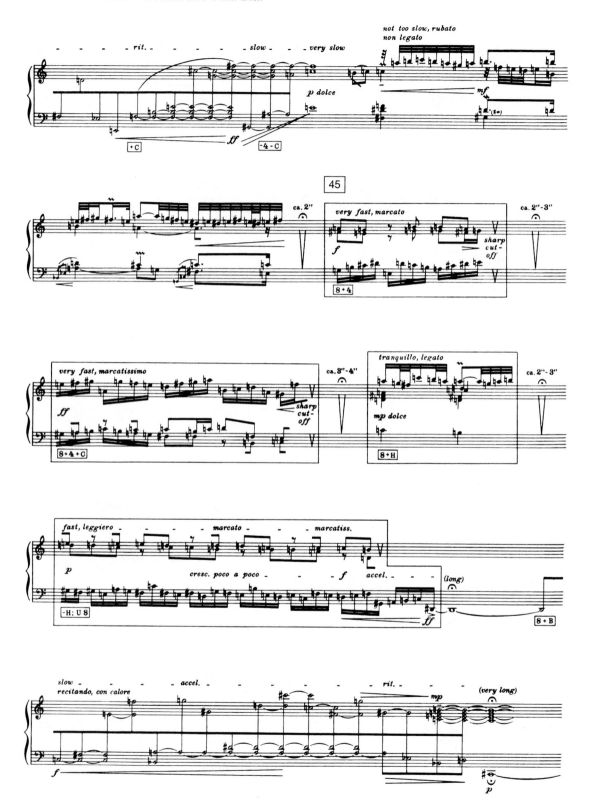

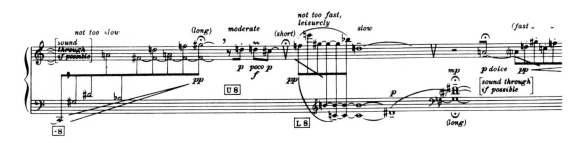

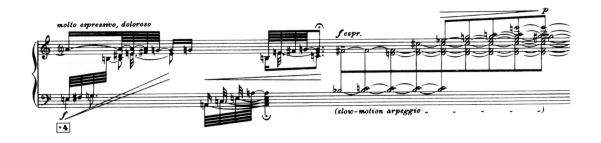

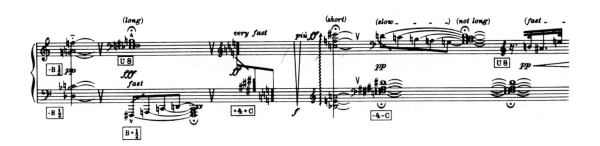

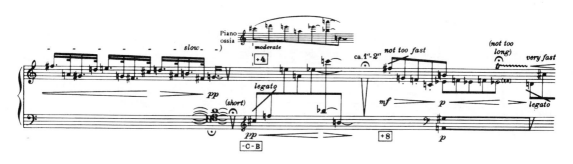

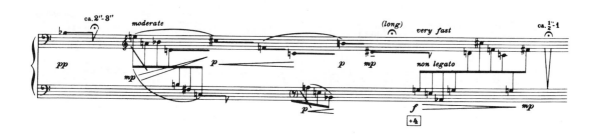

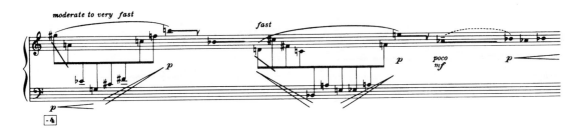

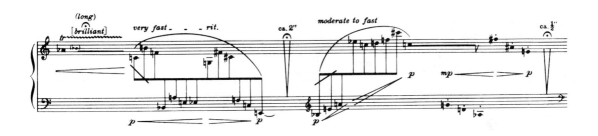

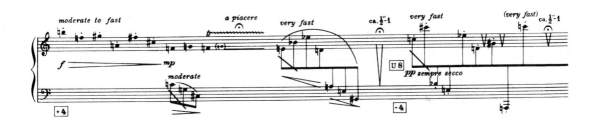

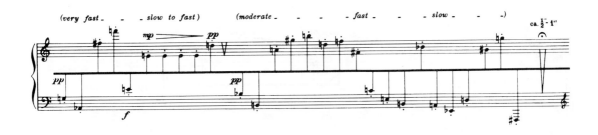

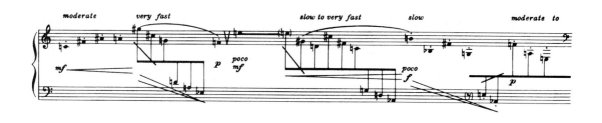

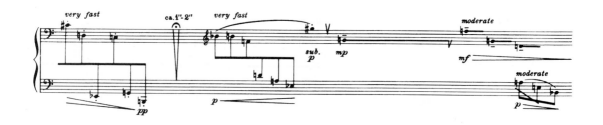

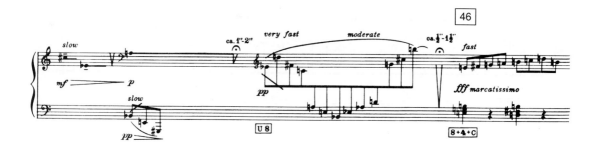

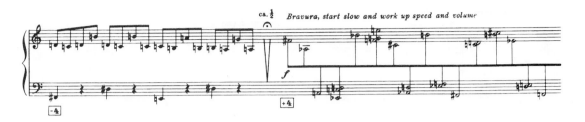

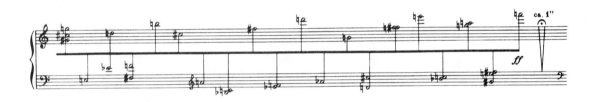

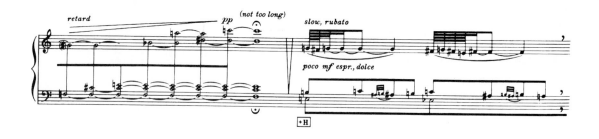

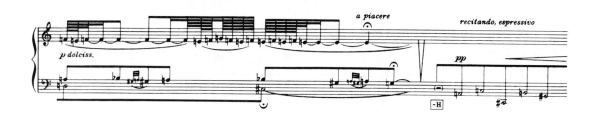

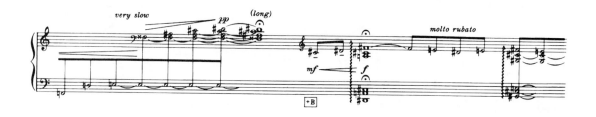

In this Fantasy for Harpsichord or Piano, composed in 1966, Rochberg adopted the style of the late Baroque toccata and quoted short passages from the Toccata in J. S. Bach's Partita in E minor, No. 6 for keyboard, BWV 830. This is not a running commentary on the Toccata, but a modern prelude inspired by and paying tribute to Bach's work. For example, Bach's Toccata contains a "Fugato a 3 voci," which is represented in Rochberg's piece only by two cryptic references to the head of the theme. Moreover, Rochberg's fantasy is notated without measure bars, like some of C. P. E. Bach's fantasies or Louis Couperin's *préludes non mesurés*.

Like Bach, Rochberg begins with an arpeggio followed by a typical double-dotted effect and a descending appoggiatura. But where Bach's arpeggio contains only the notes of the E-minor triad, Rochberg's contains all twelve notes of the chromatic scale. Similarly, the arpeggio that resolves the appoggiatura includes all of the notes of Bach's chord but in addition *B♭, E♭,* and *B.* The most characteristic trichord of the piece contains both a fourth (or fifth) and a tritone—for example, descending *A-E-B♭* and *B-F♯-C.*

Besides subtle references to gestures from Bach's piece and transfigured quotations, there are several literal quotations. These are isolated from the surrounding music by two seconds or more of silence: from measures 47, 65–66, 62–64 of the Toccata, and measure 8 from the Partita's Sarabande, which are boxed in the score, and measures 1–5 from Bach's Aria, which is not so marked.

The composer in a note to the recording stated: "While I would not place my idea of musical 'commentary' necessarily in the same category as variants or variations on another composer's theme or development sections of sonatas or chorale preludes, etc., it relates to these earlier attitudes and practices at least in the sense that something pre-existing, or 'given' is worked on, extended in new and possibly unexpected directions." (From the liner notes, Grenadilla Records GS 1019.)

Instrument Names and Abbreviations

The following tables set forth the English, Italian, German, and French names used for the various musical instruments in these scores, and their respective abbreviations.

WOODWINDS

English	Italian	German	French
Piccolo (Picc.)	Flauto piccolo (Fl. Picc.)	Kleine Flöte (Kl. Fl.)	Petite flûte
Flute (Fl.)	Flauto (Fl.); Flauto grande (Fl. gr.)	Große Flöte (Fl. gr.)	Flûte (Fl.)
Alto flute	Flauto contralto (fl.c–alto)	Altflöte	Flûte en sol
Oboe (Ob.)	Oboe (Ob.)	Hoboe (Hb.); Oboe (Ob.)	Hautbois (Hb.)
English horn (E.H.)	Corno inglese (C. or Cor. ingl., C.i.)	Englisches Horn	Cor anglais (C.A.)
Sopranino clarinet	Clarinetto piccolo (clar. picc.)		
Clarinet (C., Cl., Clt., Clar.)	Clarinetto (Cl., Clar.)	Klarinette (Kl.)	Clarinette (Cl.)
Bass clarinet (B. Cl.)	Clarinetto basso (Cl. b., Cl. basso, Clar. basso)	Bass Klarinette (Bkl.)	Clarinette basse (Cl. bs.)
Bassoon (Bsn., Bssn.)	Fagotto (Fag,. Fg.)	Fagott (Fag., Fg.)	Basson (Bssn.)
Contrabassoon (C. Bsn.)	Contrafagotto (Cfg., C. Fag., Cont. F.)	Kontrafagott (Kfg.)	Contrebasson (C. bssn.)

BRASS

English	Italian	German	French
French horn (Hr., Hn.)	Corno (Cor., C.)	Horn (Hr.) [*pl.* Hörner (Hrn.)]	Cor; Cor à pistons
Trumpet (Tpt., Trpt., Trp., Tr.)	Tromba (Tr.)	Trompete (Tr., Trp.)	Trompette (Tr.)
Trumpet in D	Tromba piccola (Tr. picc.)		
Cornet	Cornetta	Kornett	Cornet à pistons (C. à p., Pist.)
Trombone (Tr., Tbe., Trb., Trm., Trbe.)	Trombone [*pl.* Tromboni (Tbni., Trni.)]	Posaune (Ps., Pos.)	Trombone (Tr.)
Tuba (Tb.)	Tuba (Tb., Tba.)	Tuba (Tb.)	Tuba (Tb.)

PERCUSSION

English	Italian	German	French
Percussion (Perc.)	Percussione	Schlagzeug (Schlag.)	Batterie (Batt.)
Kettledrums (K. D.)	Timpani (Timp., Tp.)	Pauken (Pk.)	Timbales (Timb.)
Snare drum (S. D.)	Tamburo piccolo (Tamb. picc.)	Kleine Trommel (Kl. Tr.)	Caisse claire (C. cl.), Caisse roulante
	Tamburo militare (Tamb. milit.)		Tambour militaire (Tamb. milit.)
Bass drum (B. drum)	Gran cassa (Gr. Cassa, Gr. C., G. C.)	Große Trommel (Gr. Tr.)	Grosse caisse (Gr. c.)
Cymbals (Cym., Cymb.)	Piatti (P., Ptti., Piat.)	Becken (Beck.)	Cymbales (Cym.)
Tam-Tam (Tam-T.)			
Tambourine (Tamb.)	Tamburino (Tamb.)	Schellentrommel, Tamburin	Tambour de Basque (T. de B., Tamb. de Basque)
Triangle (Trgl., Tri.)	Triangolo (Trgl.)	Triangel	Triangle (Triang.)
Glockenspiel (Glocken.)	Campanelli (Cmp.)	Glockenspiel	Carillon
Bells (Chimes)	Campane (Cmp.)	Glocken	Cloches
Antique Cymbals	Crotali, Piatti antichi	Antiken Zimbeln	Cymbales antiques
Sleigh Bells	Sonagli (Son.)	Schellen	Grelots
Xylophone (Xyl.)	Xilofono	Xylophon	Xylophone

STRINGS

English	Italian	German	French
Violin (V., Vl., Vn., Vln., Vi.)	Violino (V., Vl., Vln.)	Violine (V., Vl., Vln.) Geige (Gg.)	Violon (V., Vl., Vln.)
Viola (Va., Vl., *pl.* Vas.)	Viola (Va., Vla.) *pl.* Viole (Vle.)	Bratsche (Br.)	Alto (A.)
Violoncello, Cello (Vcl., Vc.)	Violoncello (Vc., Vlc., Vcllo.)	Violoncell (Vc., Vlc.)	Violoncelle (Vc.)
Double bass (D. Bs.)	Contrabasso (Cb., C. B.) *pl.* Contrabassi or Bassi (C. Bassi, Bi.)	Kontrabass (Kb.)	Contrebasse (C. B.)

OTHER INSTRUMENTS

English	Italian	German	French
Harp (Hp., Hrp.)	Arpa (A., Arp.)	Harfe (Hrf.)	Harpe (Hp.)
Piano	Pianoforte (P.-f., Pft.)	Klavier	Piano
Celesta (Cel.)			
Harpsichord	Cembalo	Cembalo	Clavecin
Harmonium (Harmon.)			
Organ (Org.)	Organo	Orgel	Orgue
Guitar		Gitarre (Git.)	
Mandoline (Mand.)			

GLOSSARY

a The phrases *a 2, a 3* (etc.) indicate that the part is to be played in unison by 2, 3 (etc.) players; when a simple number (1., 2., etc.) is placed over a part, it indicates that only the first (second, etc.) player in that group should play.

abdämpfen To mute.

aber But.

accelerando (acc.) Growing faster.

accompagnato (accomp.) In a continuo part, this indicates that the chord-playing instrument resumes (*cf. tasto solo*).

adagio Slow, leisurely.

a demi-jeu Half-organ; i.e., softer registration.

ad libitum (ad lib.) An indication giving the performer liberty to: (1) vary from strict tempo; (2) include or omit the part of some voice or instrument; (3) include a cadenza of his own invention.

agitato Agitated, excited.

alla breve A time signature (¢) indicating, in the sixteenth century, a single breve per two-beat measure; in later music, the half note rather than the quarter is the unit of beat.

allargando (allarg.) Growing broader.

alle, alles All, every, each.

allegretto A moderately fast tempo (between allegro and andante).

allegro A rapid tempo (between allegretto and presto).

alto, altus (A.) The deeper of the two main divisions of women's (or boys') voices.

am Frosch At the heel (of a bow).

am Griffbrett Play near, or above, the fingerboard of a string instrument.

amoroso Loving, amorous.

am Steg On the bridge (of an instrument).

ancora Again.

andante A moderately slow tempo (between adagio and allegretto).

animato, animé Animated.

a piacere The execution of the passage is left to the performer's discretion.

arco Played with the bow.

arpeggiando, arpeggiato (arpeg.) Played in harp style, i.e., the notes of the chord played in quick succession rather than simultaneously.

assai Very.

a tempo At the (basic) tempo.

attacca Begin what follows without pausing.

auf dem On the (as in *auf dem G*, on the G string).

Auftritt Scene.

Ausdruck Expression.

ausdrucksvoll With expression.

Auszug Arrangement.

baguettes Drumsticks (*baguettes de bois, baguettes timbales de bois*, wooden drumsticks or kettledrum sticks; *baguettes d'éponge*, sponge-headed drumsticks; *baguettes midures*, semi-hard drumsticks; *baguettes dures*, hard drumsticks; *baguettes timbales en feutre*, felt-headed kettledrum sticks).

bariton Brass instrument.

bass, basso, bassus (B.) The lowest male voice.

Begleitung Accompaniment.

belebt Animated.

beruhigen To calm, to quiet.

bewegt Agitated.

bewegter More agitated.

bien Very.

breit Broadly.

breiter More broadly.

Bühne Stage.

cadenza An extended passage for solo instrument in free, improvisatory style.

calando Diminishing in volume and speed.

cambiare To change.

cantabile (cant.) In a singing style.

cantando In a singing manner.

canto Voice (as in *col canto*, a direction for the accompaniment to follow the solo part in tempo and expression).

cantus An older designation for the highest part in a vocal work.

chiuso Stopped, in horn playing.

col, colla, coll' With the.

come prima, come sopra As at first; as previously.

comme Like, as.

comodo Comfortable, easy.

con With

Continuo (Con.)   A method of indicating an accompanying part by the bass notes only, together with figures designating the chords to be played above them. In general practice, the chords are played on a lute, harpsichord or organ, while, often, a viola da gamba or cello doubles the bass notes.

contratenor   In earlier music, the name given to the third voice part which was added to the basic two-voice texture of discant and tenor, having the same range as the tenor which it frequently crosses.

corda   String; for example, *seconda (2a) corda* is the second string (the A string on the violin).

coro   Chorus.

coryphée   Leader of a ballet or chorus.

countertenor   Male alto, derived from *contratenor altus.*

crescendo (cresc.)   Increasing in volume.

da capo (D.C.)   Repeat from the beginning, usually up to the indication *Fine* (end).

daher   From there.

dal segno   Repeat from the sign.

Dämpfer (Dpf.)   Mute.

decrescendo (decresc., decr.)   Decreasing in volume.

delicato   Delicate, soft.

dessus   Treble.

détaché   With a broad, vigorous bow stroke, each note bowed singly.

deutlich   Distinctly.

diminuendo, diminuer (dim., dimin.)   Decreasing in volume.

discantus   Improvised counterpoint to an existing melody.

divisés, divisi (div.)   Divided; indicates that the instrumental group should be divided into two or more parts to play the passage in question.

dolce   Sweet and soft.

dolcemente   Sweetly.

dolcissimo (dolciss.)   Very sweet.

Doppelgriff   Double stop.

doppelt   Twice.

doppio movimento   Twice as fast.

doux   Sweet.

drängend   Pressing on.

e   And.

Echoton   Like an echo.

éclatant   Sparkling, brilliant.

einleiten   To lead into.

Encore   Again.

en dehors   Emphasized.

en fusée   Dissolving in.

erschütterung   A violent shaking, deep emotion.

espressione intensa   Intense expression.

espressivo (espress., espr.)   Expressive.

et   And.

etwas   Somewhat, rather.

expressif (express.)   Expressive.

falsetto   Male singing voice in which notes above the ordinary range are obtained artificially.

falsobordone   Four-part harmonization of psalm tones with mainly root-position chords.

fauxbourdon (faulx bourdon)   Three-part harmony in which the chant melody in the treble is accompanied by two lower voices, one in parallel sixths, and the other improvised a fourth below the melody.

fermer brusquement   To close abruptly.

fine   End, close.

flatterzunge, flutter-tongue   A special tonguing technique for wind intruments, producing a rapid trill-like sound.

flüchtig   Fleeting, transient.

fois   Time (as in *premier fois,* first time).

forte (f)   Loud.

fortissimo (ff)   Very loud (*fff* indicates a still louder dynamic).

fortsetzend   Continuing.

forza   Force.

frei   Free.

fugato   A section of a composition fugally treated.

funebre   Funereal, mournful.

fuoco   Fire, spirit.

furioso   Furious.

ganz   Entirely, altogether.

gebrochen   Broken.

gedehnt   Held back.

gemächlich   Comfortable.

Generalpause (G.P.)   Rest for the complete orchestra.

geschlagen   Struck.

geschwinder   More rapid, swift.

gesprochen   Spoken.

gesteigert   Intensified.

gestopft (chiuso)   Stopped; for the notes of a horn obtained by placing the hand in the bell.

gestrichen (gestr.)   Bowed.

gesungen   Sung.

geteilt (get.)   Divided; indicates that the instrumental group should be divided into two parts to play the passage in question.

gewöhnlich (gew., gewöhnl.)   Usual, customary.
giusto   Moderate.
gleichmässig   Equal, symmetrical.
gli altri   The others.
glissando (gliss.)   Rapidly gliding over strings or keys, producing a scale run.
grande   Large, great.
grave   Slow, solemn; deep, low.
gravement   Gravely, solemnly.
grazioso   Graceful.
groß, großes, großer, etc.   Large, big.

H⁻   *Hauptstimme,* the most important voice in the texture.
Halbe   Half.
Halt   Stop, hold.
harmonic (harm.)   A flute-like sound produced on a string instrument by lightly touching the string with the finger instead of pressing it down.
Hauptzeitmass   Original tempo.
heftiger   More passionate, violent.
hervortretend   Prominently.
Holz   Woodwinds.
hörbar   Audible.

immer   Always.
impetuoso   Impetuous, violent.
istesso tempo   The same tempo, as when the duration of the beat remains unaltered despite meter change.

klagend   Lamenting.
klangvoll   Sonorous, full-sounding.
klingen lassen   Allow to sound.
kräftig   Stong, forceful.
kurz   Short.
kurzer   Shorter.

laissez vibrer   Let vibrate; an indication to the player of a harp, cymbal, etc., that the sound must not be damped.
langsam   Slow.
langsamer   Slower.
largamente   Broadly.
larghetto   Slightly faster than largo.
largo   A very slow tempo.
lebhaft   Lively.
legato   Performed without any perceptible interruption between notes.
leggéro, leggiero (legg.)   Light and graceful.
legno   The wood of the bow (*col legno tratto,* bowed with the wood; *col legno battuto,* tapped with the wood; *col legno gestrich,* played with the wood).

leidenschaftlich   Passionate, vehement.
lent   Slow.
lentamente   Slowly.
lento   A slow tempo (between andante and largo).
l.h.   Abbreviation for "left hand."
lié   Tied.

ma   But.
maestoso   Majestic.
maggiore   Major key.
main   Hand (*droite,* right; *gauche,* left).
marcatissimo (marcatiss.)   With very marked emphasis.
marcato (mar.)   Marked, with emphasis.
marcia   March.
marqué   Marked, with emphasis.
mässig   Moderate.
mean   Middle part of a polyphonic composition.
meno   Less.
mezza voce   With half the voice power.
mezzo forte (mf)   Moderately loud.
mezzo piano (mp)   Moderately soft.
minore   In the minor mode.
minuetto   Minuet.
mit   With.
M.M.   Metronome; followed by an indication of the setting for the correct temp.
moderato, modéré   At a moderate tempo.
molto   Very, much.
mosso   Rapid.
motetus   In medieval polyphonic music, a voice part above the tenor; generally, the first additional part to be composed.
moto   Motion.
muta, mutano   Change the tuning of the instrument as specified.

N⁻   *Nebenstimme,* the second most important voice in the texture.
Nachslag   Auxiliary note (at end of trill).
nehmen (nimmt)   To take.
neue   New.
nicht, non   Not.
noch   Still, yet.

octava (okt., 8va)   Octave; if not otherwise qualified, means the notes marked should be played an octave higher than written.
ohne (o.)   Without.
open   In brass instruments, the opposite of muted. In string instruments, refers to the unstopped string (i.e., sounding at its full length).

ordinario, ordinairement (ordin., ord.)   In the usual way (generally cancelling an instruction to play using some special technique).

ôtez les sourdines   Remove the mutes.

parlando   A singing style with the voice approximating speech.

parte   Part (*colla parte,* the accompaniment is to follow the voice parts).

passione   Passion.

pause   Rest.

pedal (ped., P.)   In piano music, indicates that the damper pedal should be depressed; an asterisk indicates the point of release (brackets below the music are also used to indicate pedalling). On an organ, the pedals are a keyboard played with the feet.

perdendosi   Gradually dying away.

peu   Little, a little.

pianissimo (pp)   Very soft (*ppp* indicates a still softer dynamic).

piano (p)   Soft.

più   More.

pizzicato (pizz.)   The string plucked with the finger.

plötzlich   Suddenly, immediately.

plus   More.

pochissimo (pochiss.)   Very little.

poco   Little, a little.

poco a poco   Little by little.

ponticello (pont.)   The bridge (of a string instrument).

portato   Performance manner between legato and staccato.

prenez   Take up.

près de la table   On the harp, the plucking of the strings near the soundboard.

prestissimo   Very fast.

presto   A very quick tempo (faster than allegro).

prima   First.

principale (pr.)   Principal, solo.

quasi   Almost, as if.

quasi niente   Almost nothing, i.e., as softly as possible.

quintus   An older disignation for the fifth part in a vocal work.

rallentando (rall., rallent.)   Growing slower.

rasch   Quick.

recitative (recit.)   A vocal style designed to imitate and emphasize the natural inflections of speech.

rinforzando (rinf.)   Sudden accent on a single note or chord.

ritardando (rit., ritard.)   Gradually slackening in speed.

ritmico   Rhythmical.

rubato   A certain elasticity and flexibility of tempo, speeding up and slowing down, according to the requirements of the music.

ruhig   Calm.

ruhiger   More calmly.

saltando (salt.)   An indication to the string player to bounce the bow off the string by playing with short, quick bow-strokes.

sans   Without.

scherzando (scherz.)   Playfully.

schleppend   Dragging.

schnell   Fast.

schneller   Faster.

schon   Already.

schwerer   Heavier, more difficult.

schwermütig   Dejected, sad.

sec., secco   Dry, simple.

segno   Sign in form of .𝄌˙ indicating the beginning and end of a section to be repeated.

segue   (1) Continue to the next movement without pausing; (2) continue in the same manner.

sehr   Very.

semplice   Simple, in a simple manner.

sempre   Always, continually.

senza   Without.

senza mis[ura]   Free of regular meter.

serpent   Bass of the cornett family.

seulement   Only.

sforzando, sforzato (sfz, sf)   With sudden emphasis.

simile   In a similar manner.

sino al . . .   Up to the . . . (usually followed by a new tempo marking, or by a dotted line indicating a terminal point).

sombre   Dark, somber.

son   Sound.

sonore   Sonorous, with full tone.

sopra   Above; in piano music, used to indicate that one hand must pass above the other.

soprano (Sop., S.)   The voice with the highest range.

sordino (sord.)   Mute.

sostenendo, sostenuto (sost.)   Sustained.

sotto voce   In an undertone, subdued, under the breath.

sourdine   Mute.

soutenu   Sustained.

spiccato   With a light bouncing motion of the bow.

spirito   Spirited, lively.

spiritoso   Humorous.

sprechstimme (sprechst.)   Speaking voice.

staccato (stacc.)   Detached, separated, abruptly disconnected.

stentando, stentato (stent.)   Hesitating, retarding.

Stimme   Voice.

strepitoso, strepito   Noisy, boisterous.

stretto   In a non-fugal composition, indicates a concluding section at an increased speed.

stringendo (string.)   Quickening.

subito (sub.)   Suddenly, immediately.

sul   On the (as in *sul G.* on the G string).

suono   Sound, tone.

superius   The uppermost part.

sur   On.

Takt   Bar, beat.

tasto solo   In a continuo part, this indicates that only the string instrument plays; the chord-playing instrument is silent.

temp primo (temp I)   At the original tempo.

tendrement   Tenderly.

tenerezza   Tenderness.

tenor, tenore (T., ten.)   High male voice or part.

tenuto (ten.)   Held, sustained.

touche   Fingerboard or fret (of a string instrument).

tranquillo   Quiet, calm.

trauernd   Mournfully.

treble   Soprano voice or range.

tremolo (trem)   On string instruments, a quick reiteration of the same tone, produced by a rapid up-and-down movement of the bow; also a rapid alternation between two different notes.

très   Very.

trill (tr.)   The rapid alternation of a given note with the note above it. In a drum part it indicates rapid alternating strokes with two drumsticks.

triplum   In medieval polyphonic music, a voice part above the tenor.

tristement   Sadly.

troppo   Too much.

tutti   Literally, "all"; usually means all the instruments in a given category as distinct from a solo part.

übertönend   Drowning out.

unison (unis.)   The same notes or melody played by several instruments at the same pitch. Often used to emphasize that a phrase is not to be divided among several players.

Unterbrechung   Interruption, suspension.

veloce   Fast.

verhalten   Restrained, held back.

verklingen lassen   To let die away.

Verwandlung   Change of scene.

verzweiflungsvoll   Full of despair.

vibrato   Slight fluctuation of pitch around a sustained tone.

vif   Lively.

vigoroso   Vigorous, strong.

vivace   Quick, lively.

voce   Voice.

volti   Turn over (the page).

Vorhang auf   Curtain up.

Vorhang fällt, Vorhang zu   Curtain down.

voriges   Preceding.

vorwärts   Forward, onward.

weg   Away, beyond.

wieder   Again.

wie oben   As above, as before.

zart   Tenderly, delicately.

ziemlich   Suitable, fit.

zurückhaltend   Slackening in speed.

zurückkehrend zum   Return to, go back to.

Index of Composers

INDEX OF TITLES

INDEX OF FORMS AND GENRES

Index to NAWM References in Grout/Palisca, *A History of Western Music*, 5th Edition